Successful Business Communication In A Week

Martin Manser

The Teach Yourself series has been trusted around the world for over 60 years. This series of 'In A Week' business books is designed to help people at all levels and around the world to further their careers. Learn in a week, what the experts learn in a lifetime.

Martin Manser is a professional reference book editor. His major management experience has been in managing people and projects, including leading a team of nearly 100 people on one of the few twentieth-century study Bibles (*The Thematic Reference Bible*, Hodder and Stoughton, 1996) to be originated in the UK. He has also led teams to manage the award-winning *Collins Bible Companion* (HarperCollins, 2009) and the bestselling *Macmillan Student's Dictionary* (Macmillan, 2nd edition, 1996). Since 2001, he has been a Language Trainer and Consultant with national and international companies and organizations, leading courses on business communications, report writing, project management and time management.

Website: www.martinmanser.co.uk

Acknowledgements

I wish to thank Linda Eley for her careful typing of my manuscript.

Martin Manser

Successful Business Communication

Martin Manser

www.inaweek.co.uk

Hodder Education

338 Euston Road, London NW1 3BH.

Hodder Education is an Hachette UK company

First published in UK 2013 by Hodder Education

This edition published 2013

Copyright © 2013 Martin H. Manser

The moral rights of the author have been asserted

Database right Hodder Education (makers)

British Library Cataloguing in Publication Data: a catalogue record for this title is available from the British Library.

10 9 8 7 6 5 4 3 2 1

The publisher has used its best endeavours to ensure that any website addresses referred to in this book are correct and active at the time of going to press. However, the publisher and the author have no responsibility for the websites and can make no guarantee that a site will remain live or that the content will remain relevant, decent or appropriate.

The publisher has made every effort to mark as such all words which it believes to be trademarks. The publisher should also like to make it clear that the presence of a word in the book, whether marked or unmarked, in no way affects its legal status as a trademark.

Every reasonable effort has been made by the publisher to trace the copyright holders of material in this book. Any errors or omissions should be notified in writing to the publisher, who will endeavour to rectify the situation for any reprints and future editions.

Hachette UK's policy is to use papers that are natural, renewable and recyclable products and made from wood grown in sustainable forests. The logging and manufacturing processes are expected to conform to the environmental regulations of the country of origin.

www.hoddereducation.co.uk

Typeset by Cenveo Publisher Services.

Printed in Great Britain by CPI Group (UK) Ltd, Croydon, CR0 4YY

Contents

Introduction

We live in an age when the number of ways in which we communicate in business is constantly increasing. Years ago, we simply had face-to-face communication, phone and letter. Now we also have more, including email, websites, blogs ... and yet, if we're honest, alongside this increase in the ways in which we communicate has come a decrease in the level of effective communication.

How familiar are you with the following?

Working relationships that show low levels of trust

'There's too much information and I can't "see the wood for the trees"'

Colleagues who talk only in jargon that no one understands

The minutes of a meeting are unclear

PowerPoint presentations that have too many points but are vague in their core message

Unfortunately, the list could easily go on. We are all too aware of poor communication at all levels in business. What can we do? I've written this book to offer some positive guidelines to help *you* communicate more effectively. You may not be able to change the way your company or organization works, but you can change the way in which *you* work.

So we'll explore the following:

Sunday: Know your aims. Who are you writing to? What is your message? What response do you want those you are communicating with to make?

Monday: Listen carefully as colleagues explain the challenges they are facing. When you listen, you show you value your colleagues as individuals.

Tuesday: Write clearly. Think creatively about what you want to express, organize your thoughts and then draft and edit your email or report.

Wednesday: Organize better meetings. The key to a successful meeting lies in its preparation, especially why you are holding it, who needs to be present and what you will consider.

Thursday: Give successful presentations. Prepare well, knowing your audience and your key messages, backed up if necessary by useful visual aids.

Friday: Build strong working relationships. Good working relationships are the glue that holds an organization together. How can you cultivate stronger working relationships?

Saturday: Engage effectively online by building – and maintaining – an accessible website and networking by means of social media.

Each day of the week covers a different area and the material begins with an introduction as to what the day is about. Then comes the main material that explains the key lessons by clarifying important principles which are backed up by tips, case studies, etc. Each day concludes with a summary, exercise and multiple-choice questions, to reinforce the learning points.

The principles I outline here are the fruit of over 30 years in business, particularly in the area of writing, and over ten years in leading courses on business communications. As I have reflected on participants' responses to the workshops I have led, two comments keep recurring: 'You gave me more confidence' and 'The workshop was a refresher course'. My hope therefore is that, as you read and act on what I write, it will be a refresher course that will give you fresh confidence to be a more effective communicator at work.

Martin Manser

SUNDAY

Know your aims

Today we're going to look at:

- basic aims in communicating: if we know where we are going, we are more likely to arrive at our destination than if we wander aimlessly.
- different ways in which people learn: one of the key themes of this book is to make sure that our communication is focused not on ourselves but on the person we want to communicate with. If that is so, we need to make sure our message is expressed in the way that is most appropriate for them.
- various ways in which you can communicate: another of the key themes of this book is that there is more to business communication than just typing an email and then pressing 'send'. We'll therefore explore some of these different ways of communicating here and later in the week, e.g. better working relationships (Monday and Friday); writing effective reports and emails (Tuesday); holding better meetings (Wednesday); giving powerful presentations (Thursday); building accessible websites (Saturday).
- some barriers in communication ... and how we can overcome them.

SUNDAY

MONDAY

TUESDAY

WEDNESDAY

THURSDAY

FRIDAY

SATURDAY

The basics of communication

I often begin my workshops on communication with the memory prompt **AIR:**

- Audience
- Intention
- Response

There is more to business communication than just typing an email and then pressing 'send'.

Audience

'Audience' means know who you want to communicate with. Here the focus is not on you, but on the person/people you are trying to communicate with. This means the question you should ask yourself is *not* so much 'What should I say/write?' but 'What does my audience need to hear?' To answer that question well, you need to think about who your audience is and what their response to your communication is likely to be.

For example, if you are writing a document, the person who you are writing to should affect the way in which you write. Are you writing to your boss or to someone who has written to your company or organization with a complaint? In each case, how you express what you are trying to say will be different.

If you are emailing your boss, you may simply give him or her the information that he or she has asked for:

> Hi Robert:
>
> Sales for 2012 were 10% up on 'Introduction to Project Management'. We have sold just over 3,000 copies and we reprinted a further 1,000 copies of that title last month.
>
> Harry

Your boss wants the information quickly, with no extras. If you are responding to a complaint, however, your tone will be different:

Dear Mrs Brown,

Thank you for taking the trouble to write to us to express your dissatisfaction with the service you recently received at one of our restaurants. I am very sorry that you found our service unsatisfactory.

I have checked the details from your letter and it appears that the member of staff you dealt with on 3 October in Grantchester was a temporary worker. He was unfamiliar with our company policy on the high levels of service we require from all our staff.

I have now taken the necessary steps to ensure that such a situation will not occur again.

Thank you again for writing. Please be assured that we aim to offer our customers the highest possible level of service at all times.

Yours sincerely

John Duckworth

Do you see the difference? The email to your boss is short and to the point. The letter responding to the complaint is expanded and also, crucially, the *tone* is much softer.

So you need to know who your audience is. When I am preparing a talk, I will often think of one or two people I know who will be in the audience, and I gauge how they are likely to receive what I am saying, their present level of understanding and the point I want them to reach by the end of my talk.

Intention

By 'Intention' I mean the message: the key point(s) you want to put over. In the above examples, the key points to your boss are stated very briefly, and the intention in replying to the person who complained was to defuse their anger and say that you had looked into the matter.

You may face some difficulties in identifying what the intention/message of your communication is.

You may not know it yourself. If this is the case, *think*. To take an example, my website was recently down and I was without one, so it made me think, 'What is the purpose of my website? Do I want people simply to find out about me and my services or to buy books from me or to contact me with questions?' Think hard until you can identify your key messages definitely and precisely. We will explore more on this crucial area of thinking and the role of mind maps or pattern notes on Tuesday.

Is your message clear? If it isn't clear to you, then it will hardly be clear to those you are trying to communicate with. On one of my courses I discovered that the key message of one document was in a 67-word sentence in brackets near the end of the document!

Even if you do know what your key message is, you may need to explain some background to that key message before you can get to it.

TIP

If your message isn't clear to you, then it will not be clear to those you are trying to communicate with.

Introducing change

John was hired by Denton Manufacturing Company to introduce change. There was a culture of 'we've always done it this way – why do we need to change?' in the company, but its traditional outlook meant that it was being overtaken fast by smaller, newer firms. He gathered his fellow directors and senior staff on an awayday. His first task was to enable his colleagues to see the weaknesses in their present way of working and to create a sense of dissatisfaction that would lead them to want to change. Because John identified his primary message clearly, he could focus on that as a successful first step in introducing change.

Response

What do you want the person you are communicating with to do with your communication? Sometimes we can be so preoccupied with working out all the details of what we are trying to say that we forget what we want our readers, for example, to do with the information we give them. You may be writing to them simply to inform the people you are writing to – but it is more likely that you want them to make some decision.

Is it crystal clear how they are to respond? What are the next steps you want them to take? For example, suppose you are writing a fundraising email. You need to include in clear terms which website your readers can donate money on, giving bank account codes as necessary, and how donors can gift-aid their contributions.

Different ways of learning

Every individual is different and, if we want to communicate effectively with a range of individuals, we would be wise to try to discover their preferred learning style. There are three main learning styles:

- **visual** – those who like to see information in the written word, pictures or diagrams to take it in well

- **auditory** – those who learn by listening to information
- **kinaesthetic** – those who learn by actively doing things, e.g. by role play.

It can be very useful for you to discern where your own personal preference lies. I am more visual and auditory rather than kinaesthetic. The aim here is to challenge your assumption that the way in which other people learn is the same as how you learn. You need this reminder that other people's learning styles will be different from yours. To be an effective communicator, you therefore need to be alert to the styles of those you want to communicate with.

You can discern others' styles from how they respond and you can then at least use these words as indicators of their style, for example:

- **visual** – *see, look, picture, focus*
- **auditory** – *hear* ('I hear what you're saying'), *buzz, rings a bell*
- **kinaesthetic** – *feel, concrete, get to grips with, contact.*

Different methods of communication

You can use your knowledge of the different styles in which people learn to find the best way to communicate with them. To communicate most effectively, you should send your communication in the form that is most suited to your audience. We can therefore immediately see that email will not be useful for everyone in all circumstances. For auditory learners, a phone call may well be more effective; for kinaesthetic learners, a meeting that puts suggestions into action will help.

We can also distinguish some groups further. For example, among visual learners, some will respond more to words, others to pictures or diagrams. This has significance. To give two examples: (1) If I am preparing a PowerPoint presentation, I will not simply list headings in words but I will also work hard to find a picture that encapsulates the key idea visually. This can be very time-consuming, but I am sure it is worth it.

(An example: a picture of buttresses supporting a cathedral to communicate the concepts of strengthening and confirming.) (2) When preparing a map, not only give directions ('After five miles on the A21, at the roundabout, turn left...') but also draw a map with lines in a diagram.

The two approaches (words and picture/diagram) in examples 1 and 2 reflect the fact that one approach (words or picture/diagram) will appeal to some but not to others. By combining two approaches I hope to reach many more people than I would have done if I had followed only one approach.

Making an informal contract

Peter had to commission several university lecturers to write a series of books for the publishing company he worked for.

As he began to email prospective authors Peter quickly realized that some responded to emails but many did not. Later, as he met up with those he was going to commission and began to work more closely with them, he deliberately made an informal contract with them. He asked them which communication method (e.g. email or phone) they preferred and, especially if by phone, what days/times were best for them to be contacted. Having this knowledge meant that his frustration at their lack of response was significantly less than if he did not have such information and so his communication with his writers was more effective.

Email is very useful for communicating information, quick checks and seeking quick agreement. It is weak, however, in building good business relationships. For more on writing emails, see **Tuesday.**

Phone calls are useful for discussions, because you can discern immediately whether or not someone has understood what you are trying to say. Unless you have a way of screening phone calls, however, they can interrupt your work. So it can be useful (1) to arrange in advance a convenient time to call or

(2) to ask at the beginning of a call 'Is now a convenient time to talk?'

Be aware that your mood will often be detected by the person you are speaking to on the phone. Without being able to see the person you are speaking to, we tend to build up a mental picture of them. As far as you can, convey enthusiasm as you talk. One way that is often recommended is to smile as you speak.

Before making an important call, jot down the points you want to discuss. How often do we not do that, only to finish the call and then realize we have not discussed something important?

It can also be useful to signal the scope of the call at the beginning ('Ray, I think there are three areas we need to discuss today.') Unless the matters are sensitive, aim to discuss the most important matter first, in case either party cannot continue talking and has to finish the call quickly. If one of the matters is sensitive, then you can ease yourself into tackling it by discussing less significant matters first and then proceeding to the more delicate one.

If you are trying to persuade a colleague to do something, before you begin the call list to yourself the possible objections they might raise and deal with each one. In this way you will be prepared for what they will say.

Don't be afraid of summarizing where you have got to at a certain point in a phone call ('OK, so we've agreed quantities and delivery dates, now let's move on to prices').

Face-to-face meetings are more expensive but are indispensable in business. As we email and phone colleagues around the world we probably build up a mental picture of their appearance and manner – and when, perhaps much later, we meet them our perceptions may well be proved wrong. When two people meet face to face in such circumstances, one may well say to the other, 'It is good to put a face to a name.' Face-to-face meetings also often provide opportunities for more informal relationship building; during a mid-morning break or lunch we can discuss our colleague's family or holiday plans, for example. For more on meetings, see **Wednesday** and, on building stronger working relationships, see **Friday.**

Barriers in communication

We conclude Sunday by looking at barriers to effective communication.

What is effective communication? I often present it like this:

This means that A wants to communicate content A (whatever it is), represented by a triangle. What we want B to receive and understand is a triangle, not a square, circle or a partially formed triangle.

So what prevents effective communication from taking place? What are some of the barriers to good communication and how can they be resolved?

- Your presentation is poorly focused, unclear and vague. Resolve by preparing well and being clear and precise (see also **Tuesday** and **Thursday**).
- You give too little information. Resolve by knowing your audience better and knowing the amount of information they need to make a decision.

SUNDAY

MONDAY

TUESDAY

WEDNESDAY

THURSDAY

FRIDAY

SATURDAY

- You give too much unnecessary detail and too much information. Resolve by knowing your audience better and knowing the amount of information they need to make a decision.
- You use incomprehensible words and phrases. Every business has its own jargon and set of abbreviations. Resolve by using only those terms that you know your audience can understand.

- The person you are trying to communicate with is significantly less able to communicate in your language. Resolve by being far simpler in what you are trying to communicate; see also **Tuesday** and **Thursday.**
- Inaccurate information undermines the credibility of the rest of what you want to communicate. Resolve by checking your facts first.
- You have negative feelings towards certain individuals; for example, someone may be perceived as too abrupt and insensitive. We devote two days (**Monday** and **Friday**) to dealing with this.
- You lack trust in a person: their words may sound right but you don't believe them. Credibility is gained and kept not only by someone's knowledge and expertise but also by the relationship you have with that person. See **Monday** and **Friday** for hints on dealing with this.
- The politics and/or processes of your company or organization may hinder good communication. For example, I recently heard of an organization running a conference whose management released details of the speaker and

other essential details *to their own staff* only three weeks before the conference was due to take place!

- Formal channels of communication in a business setting are unclear and colleagues rely on unofficial means of communication ('the grapevine') for information, which will include rumours rather than facts. Resolve by being more decisive and, probably, more open about communicating. See also **Monday** and **Friday.**

- The approach is badly timed. For example, asking for an immediate decision on an important matter that requires much thought should be done at a time that is appropriate. Resolve by finding out and planning what that appropriate time is.

- Your body language is in conflict with your message. For example you may try to sound friendly but your awkward posture and lack of eye contact with the person you are speaking to express your attitude more fully. See also **Thursday** and **Friday.**

- In meetings, you allow the discussion to wander. On this and other deficiencies in meetings, see **Wednesday.**

Summary

Today we've looked at knowing the basics of communication. In particular, it is essential that you are aware of AIR: (A) your audience, who you are trying to communicate with; (I) your intention/message, what you are trying to communicate; (R) the response you are trying to gain from the person you are communicating with.

In considering who our audience is, we considered the style in which they best learn. We distinguished *visual, auditory* and *kinaesthetic* styles and can use that as a basis to determine the most appropriate way in which we can communicate with them.

Exercise

1 Think of a good piece of communication that you have been involved in. Why was it successful?
   A Who was the audience: who were you communicating with?
   I Intention: what was your message? What were you trying to say?
   R Response: what response did you receive?
   ● Why was it successful? How do you know?

SUNDAY

MONDAY

TUESDAY

WEDNESDAY

THURSDAY

FRIDAY

SATURDAY

2 Think of a bad piece of communication that you have been involved in. Why was it not successful?

A Who was the audience: who were you communicating with?

I Intention: what was your message? What were you trying to say?

R Response: what response did you receive?

● Why was it not successful? How do you know?

Fact-check (answers at the back)

1. To stop and think about what exactly you are trying to communicate is:
   a) a luxury ❑
   b) a nice to have ❑
   c) essential ❑
   d) a waste of time. ❑

2. Effective communication needs:
   a) spontaneity ❑
   b) no planning ❑
   c) improvisation ❑
   d) thought and planning. ❑

3. Thinking about the basics of communication, the letters AIR stand for:
   a) Abbreviations, Image, Reputation ❑
   b) Activity, Information, Reflection ❑
   c) Audience, Intention, Response ❑
   d) Attachments, Internet, Receptivity. ❑

4. Clarifying who you are communicating to is:
   a) vital ❑
   b) a waste of time ❑
   c) unnecessary ❑
   d) quite important. ❑

5. What you are trying to communicate should be:
   a) vague ❑
   b) clear ❑
   c) confusing ❑
   d) ambiguous. ❑

6. You've forgotten to think about what response you want from the information in an email you're about to send. Should you:
   a) press send, knowing they can email back if they want to pursue it? ❑
   b) rewrite the email before you press 'send'? ❑
   c) hope that the recipient will not notice? ❑
   d) tell your boss about it tomorrow? ❑

7. 'Everyone learns in the same way as I do' is:
   a) always false ❑
   b) always true ❑
   c) true sometimes ❑
   d) false sometimes. ❑

8. Email is the best way to communicate in business.
   a) always true ❑
   b) sometimes true ❑
   c) false ❑
   d) true ❑

9. Telephoning business contacts is good:
   a) for socializing ❑
   b) for finding out about your competitors ❑
   c) for developing better working relationships ❑
   d) only when your email is down. ❑

10. 'There are so many barriers to effective communication that I feel like giving up now.'
a) Yes – leave work early and don't come back. ❏
b) 'Sorry, what did you say?' ❏
c) 'I'll think about it and come back to you later on it.' ❏
d) No – that's all the more reason to listen well, develop good business relationships and work hard. ❏

MONDAY

Listen carefully

When thinking about communication, we tend immediately to think of speaking or writing. However, before we can consider those, we need to remember that our communication is not isolated from its context. We speak or write in certain situations, and listening carefully has to come before speaking or writing to enable what we say or write to be effective.

So today we consider:

- the importance of listening
- how to listen more attentively, focusing on what the other person is saying
- steps to help us listen more effectively.

In contrast to speaking and writing, which are productive skills, listening is a receptive skill. Later today, we will also look at the other receptive skill, reading, and suggest ways in which we can improve our techniques for reading texts and statistics.

Listen more attentively

The comments today focus on listening in face-to-face relationships. As a manager, you will be expected to do a lot of listening: to your boss as he/she directs your work, to colleagues as you talk about your work, in meetings as you discuss a range of subjects and make decisions (see also **Wednesday**), and as you interview staff, solve problems and use the phone (look back at **Sunday**).

I'M A VERY GOOD LISTENER

Listening is hard work

There are many reasons why listening is difficult:

- We tend to focus on what we want to say; by contrast, listening demands that our concentration is on someone else as we follow the sequence of their thoughts.
- The person we're listening to may speak unclearly, too fast or repeat himself/herself.
- The person we're listening to may be a non-native speaker and so does not speak in standard English.

- We were probably not taught to listen. I vaguely remember school lessons trying to teach us reading, writing and speaking but I don't think I was ever taught to listen (or maybe I wasn't listening during those lessons!).

But listening is a really valuable skill. Have you ever felt really burdened by something and opened your heart to someone else? At the end you feel relieved and can say, 'Thank you for listening.'

 Listening is far more than merely hearing.

The importance of listening

Listening:

- focuses on the other person. Often when someone else is talking, we're focusing on thinking about what we are going to say as a reply.
- values the person you are listening to as an individual in their own right, so that you understand 'where they're coming from', why they are working or speaking as they are.
- helps you understand the point at which a person is. For example, if you are trying to sell something to customers, you want to build a good relationship with them. By listening, you will discern who is interested and who is not, so you can use your time more valuably and concentrate on the likelier potential clients.
- encourages you to ask the right questions. As you focus on the other person (not yourself), you will want to know more. We can distinguish:
  - closed questions: ones that can be answered by a straight 'Yes' or 'No': 'Was the project late?' 'Yes.' 'Will you be able to give me the figures by 5.00 p.m.?' 'No.'
  - open questions: ones that get people talking. Open questions begin with why, how, who, when, where, what. 'Why do you think the project is running late?' 'Because we did not plan enough time for the extra work the

customer now wants.' Most of the questions you should ask as a manager should be open questions.

- means that you do not listen only to the words a colleague is speaking: you can perceive their response to what you are saying by being sensitive to their body language and tone of voice.
- allows you to 'listen between the lines', to become aware of any underlying messages – your response could be, for example, 'So I guess what you're saying is that you need someone else to help you complete this task on time.'
- allows you to distinguish between facts and opinions. You will hear both, and you can discern what is objective information and what are the subjective thoughts on such information. You are then in a position to evaluate what has been said.
- enables you to gather information so that you can solve problems and make decisions more efficiently.
- builds trust between people: you show that you are genuinely interested in them. This forms the basis to help you work well with them. Listening often improves relationships. Rather than someone keeping angry feelings to himself/herself and becoming increasingly tense, listening – and allowing someone to speak openly about his/her difficulties – provides a release for them.
- offers an opportunity to develop more all-round relationships. For example, if a colleague says, 'I'm off on holiday tomorrow,' you can either ignore that signal (but ignoring it is possibly slightly rude) or you can use that as a hint that they want to tell you more about themselves: 'Great, where are you going to?' 'Hong Kong.' You can then remember to ask them 'How was Hong Kong?' when you next see them.
- can resolve disagreements. If colleagues are in conflict with one another, listening to, and understanding, the opinions of the other side – not necessarily agreeing with them – is an important first step in settling a disagreement.
- helps you understand people better. As you listen carefully to someone, you will discover more about that person: what is important to them, how they think and what they are feeling.

Recently a stressed-out colleague told me, 'I want to go back to Australia.' That seemed to tell me a lot about her: a desire to be released from present tensions and return to a former, more relaxed environment. Having such knowledge helps you work better with them, even if you don't like them or agree with their opinions.

Susie was angry

Susie was angry. She worked late every evening to complete her tasks in the project but she felt her work was not appreciated or valued. It was only when a new colleague, Jan, started to work alongside her that something happened. Jan was concerned less about herself and her own work (which she did well) and more about her colleague; she cared enough to stop and listen to Susie. Susie was in tears as she poured out her heart to Jan, telling her about the real pressures she was working under. At the end of their conversation Susie told Jan, 'Thanks for listening. You're the first person I've been able to talk to about these things.'

Tips on better listening

Here are some ways to help you improve your listening skills:

- Be responsible. Realize that listening is an active skill and as such is hard work. Concentrate. For example, when I meet someone for the first time, I listen particularly attentively to catch their name. If I think I've heard it accurately, I'll say it back to them, for instance 'Great to meet you, Nick!' If I didn't hear their name properly, I'll say, 'I'm sorry I didn't quite catch your name' or ask (if it is unusual to me and seems difficult to spell) 'Could you spell that for me, please?' (The first time I met the girl who became my wife I spelt her name correctly and was the first person she had met to do so!)
- Focus on the other person, not yourself. Don't be tempted to interrupt the other person while he/she is talking. Stop and really listen to what the other person is saying. Make eye

contact with him/her. Be interested in him/her. Rephrase what he/she has said in your own way to help you clarify the meaning in your own mind; for example, 'So what you're really saying is that we should have put in place more effective monitoring controls.' Such a rephrasing process is called 'reflective listening'.

- Be willing to accept the reasoning and opinions of others as valid. Be willing to acknowledge that you may make false assumptions and may have prejudices.
- Don't be so critical that you make an immediate decision about someone based on their appearance, their style of presentation or your first impression of their personality.
- Discern the main points of what is being said. Speakers may or may not structure their argument well. Often, in informal talks or meetings it can be difficult to distinguish between facts, opinions, examples and ideas, but try to work out the speaker's main point(s).
- Do your best to remain attentive, even if the other person is not; don't become distracted.
- Write down in note form what a speaker is saying if you need to remember what he/she is saying and you might otherwise forget it. Making notes can help you concentrate and avoid the sense that 'things go in one ear and out of the other'.
- Don't be afraid of silence. Silence is part of a conversation. It can be:
  - a junction: which way will a conversation turn?
  - a time to catch up and digest what has been said
  - an opportunity for the other person to express their thoughts further
  - an opportunity to reflect on what has been said.

Read more effectively

So far today, we've thought about listening. The other receptive skill in communication is reading. As a manager you will have a lot of material to read, for example emails, reports, websites, professional literature, contracts, technical manuals.

How do you read?

It can be helpful to stop and reflect on the way in which you read. Do you:

- pronounce the words in your head as you read?
- go over every word in every sentence?
- read through a piece of writing quickly to see which parts are important and then go back to those parts again?
- stop at words you don't understand and so make very slow progress through a long piece of writing?

Here are some guidelines to help you read more effectively:

- Decide on your aims in reading a particular text. Do you want to simply check a fact, gain an overall sense of a text, grasp a detailed knowledge of a subject (for example for a report or presentation you have to prepare) or evaluate the writer's arguments and views?

- Vary the speed at which you read a text, depending on the kind of text you are reading. Spend more time on important and/or difficult parts of the text and less time on less important and/or easier parts.
- Try not to mouth words as you read them. Mouthing words in this way not only slows you down but also means that you focus on the words rather than their meaning.

● Read more widely. (At school, we were constantly encouraged to do this, but I can't remember being told why. For the reason why reading is good, see the rest of this paragraph.) Don't just read material for work. Read a newspaper or magazine (hard copy or digital). It can help if you read material on a subject that interests you, as your motivation will be higher. Choose an article. Read it once for sense, and a second time to look at the language used. Recently I did this with some students whose use of prepositions was weak, so in the article we were reading I pointed out: *the results* **of** *the survey*; **at** *fault*; *responsible* **for**. Almost unconsciously you will pick up new words and phrases. Consult a dictionary (again, either as hard copy or online) for certain words that you do not know.

● For some important work, take notes of what you have read (see earlier today for comments on taking notes in listening). Summarizing the author's argument in your own words can be a particularly useful tool.
● If you want to undertake a more detailed read of part of a text:
  – Find out which sections of the text you want to read. Consult the table of contents/list of chapters or index. Survey or scan the text to get a wider view of it. As you do that, you will begin to see the writer's key words and phrases.

- Look out for the signposts: the introduction and conclusions; the words *firstly*, *secondly*; the beginning of paragraphs; such expressions as *on the one hand* and *on the other hand*. These guide you to see the structure of the text and can be helpful to your understanding.
- Focus on the key words and, even more important, key phrases. There is less need to concentrate on such functional grammatical words as *the, of, has, be* and a greater need to concentrate on significant words.
- Reword the main points in your mind, on computer or on paper. Express the author's key points in your own way. This will help increase your understanding.
- Think about the author's argument: do you agree with him/her? Does the text make assumptions that you disagree with? Ask questions of the text and see if they are answered. Engage your mind.
- At the end of reading, see if you can recall the main points or, even better, see if you can explain the main points to someone else. You could even review what you have read later to check that you still recall it.

The following text concerns the evaluation stage at the end of a project. The key words and phrases to concentrate on in reading are in bold:

Identify what you have achieved. Specifically, **list** what you have delivered:

- The project was built on a **solid foundation.**
- You received **strong support** from your **Project Sponsor.**
- You delivered the **desired output** in terms of the **products, services**, etc.
- **Outputs achieved** the agreed **quality standards.**
- The **actual expenditure** was **on track** compared with the **original budget.**
- **Return on investment** was **good**. The **benefits** that your company received from the project are **greater** than the **costs** incurred.
- The **actual time** taken compared well with the **original schedule:** you delivered the outcomes **on time.**

- **Robust control procedures** were in place to **track** and **monitor costs** and **schedules effectively.**
- **Customers/users** and other stakeholders were **satisfied** with the project's **outcomes.**

Effective reading ... and good time management

As a manager, Sarah was methodical about her reading. She checked her emails only a few times a day, dealing with essential matters as they arose. She didn't bother to check the many junk emails she received but simply deleted them.

She allocated Friday mornings, when she knew she generally received fewer emails, to important, but not urgent, reading material that enabled her to do her job more effectively.

As she was preparing to relax for the weekend on Friday afternoons, she read non-urgent but useful material that kept her up to date with other trends in the industry which were not directly related to her job but developed her wider professional knowledge.

Of course, sometimes very urgent matters arose, which meant that she could not always keep to this methodical time allocation, so in such cases she was flexible. Generally, however, Sarah was able to allot sufficient resources of time to reading what was useful and essential and to manage her time well.

Reading statistics

Here are some guidelines on reading and understanding numbers presented in tables:

- Check the basics: the dates covered, the sources used, the scale used, the context of the figures – for example, if the figures represent a sample, how large is that sample? Are the assumptions reasonable? Are certain figures omitted? Why? Check the definitions of terms used. Are they sound? If percentages are shown, percentages of what?

- Take one row or column and think through its content and implications to understand the data.
- Compare figures in columns and see if you can discern any patterns in the data. Consider any trends: do the numbers show a consistent pattern that increases or decreases? For instance, is actual expenditure consistently higher than budgeted?
- Consider averages. Calculate the average for a particular row or column and see what variations and exceptions there are. Try to work out reasons for such differences, e.g. variations because of higher or lower income or differing levels of employment.
- Read the text that accompanies the data and check you agree with it; be particularly wary of such expressions as 'significant' or 'these figures of course show'.
- Be careful about putting too much confidence in extrapolations of data that assume a trend will continue.

Summary

Today we've considered listening and reading, the receptive skills in communication. Improving your listening skills will mean that, when you come to speak, you will know more about who you are talking to and so you can choose your words more accurately and therefore be more effective.

Improving your reading skills will mean that you will know why you are reading a certain passage and so you can focus your energies more appropriately.

Exercise

1 Ask colleagues whether they think you are a good listener or not. Listen [!] to their response.
2 Think about a recent business conversation. Were you too busy thinking about what to say that you did not really listen to the person you were talking to?
3 What steps can you take to improve your listening skills? Be ruthlessly practical with yourself.
4 As you have read today's text, what struck you as new? What action will you take as a result of your reading?

SUNDAY
MONDAY
TUESDAY
WEDNESDAY
THURSDAY
FRIDAY
SATURDAY

Fact-check (answers at the back)

1. The key skill in listening is:
   a) looking at a person's face ❏
   b) thinking about what you want to say ❏
   c) focusing on what the other person is saying ❏
   d) looking at the floor. ❏

2. Good listening:
   a) develops worse relationships ❏
   b) provokes arguments ❏
   c) relaxes people ❏
   d) develops better working relationships. ❏

3. Listening is:
   a) easy – that's why I'm the manager ❏
   b) hard work, but rewarding ❏
   c) not worth bothering about ❏
   d) useful if you have the time. ❏

4. When I listen well, I:
   a) can discern the main points someone is trying to communicate ❏
   b) am confused ❏
   c) get easily distracted ❏
   d) interrupt the other person. ❏

5. Listening provides a basis for me to:
   a) express my own opinion to anyone who will listen ❏
   b) direct what I want to say more accurately ❏
   c) decide what to eat for lunch ❏
   d) work out who I like and who I don't. ❏

6. When I read:
   a) I read everything fast ❏
   b) I read everything slowly ❏
   c) I decide why I am reading something and use that as a basis to work out my approach ❏
   d) I question why I have to read it. ❏

7. To make sure I understand a difficult passage:
   a) I read it through quickly and hope for the best ❏
   b) I read it through slowly and hope for the best ❏
   c) I learn it off by heart, although I'm not sure I grasp its meaning ❏
   d) I take notes, summarizing the author's message in my own words. ❏

8. In reading I focus on:
   a) why I disagree with the author ❏
   b) the middle of paragraphs ❏
   c) the key phrases, especially at the beginning of paragraphs ❏
   d) the page numbers. ❏

9. I read other material outside my subject field:
   a) never ❏
   b) not at all, I'm too busy to do that ❏
   c) often ❏
   d) very rarely. ❏

10. When I read numbers in a table:
a) I focus on what regular patterns I can see between the columns ❑
b) I get hopelessly lost ❑
c) I never read numbers ❑
d) I always extrapolate the figures to see where they lead. ❑

SUNDAY

MONDAY

TUESDAY

WEDNESDAY

THURSDAY

FRIDAY

SATURDAY

TUESDAY

Write clearly

Expressing yourself clearly is essential to communicating effectively and today we're going to look at the steps you need to take to express yourself clearly in writing.

First of all, we will consider general principles of writing, which apply especially to longer documents, and then we will consider specific media of writing: emails, letters and reports.

We can break down the writing process into different steps:

- thinking
- organizing
- writing your first draft
- editing your draft.

It is important to note that there are different steps; it isn't simply a matter of typing an email with the first thing that comes into your mind and then pressing 'send'!

The writing process

Thinking

Think about what you want to write. One good way of helping you start thinking what to write is to draw a pattern diagram (also known as a mind map). Take a blank piece of A4 paper. Arrange it in landscape position and write the subject matter of the report in the middle. (Write a word or few words, but not a whole sentence.) You may find it helpful to work in pencil, as you can rub out what you write if necessary.

Now write around your central word(s) the different key aspects that come to your mind, maybe as a result of your reading. You don't need to list ideas in order of importance; simply write them down. To begin with, you don't need to join the ideas up with lines linking connected items.

If you get stuck at any point, ask yourself the question words *why, how, what, who, when, where* and *how much*. These may well set you thinking.

When I do this, I am often amazed at: (1) How easy the task is; it doesn't feel like work! The ideas and concepts seem to flow naturally and spontaneously. (2) How valuable that piece of paper is. I have captured all (or at least some or many) of the key points. I don't want to lose that piece of paper!

An example of a pattern diagram for a report on buying new computer systems is:

Users
Which company departments will use the system?

Accounts department
• Will they move over to new system?
• They introduced new system only 6 months ago

Cost
• Budget
• Check figures with Finance Director

Time available
Should be ready for 1 January

Locations
• On company's two sites

IT department
• Who will build the new system?
• Who will install the new system?

(New computer system)

Old system
• Keeps crashing
• Secure?
• Software: out of date
• Slow, constant problems

Kinds of computers
• Laptops
• iPads
• Latest technology
• How long intended to last?

Link with Intranet

Website maintenance

Security
• Privacy policy

Organizing

After you have completed the thinking stages with a pattern diagram, there are two further stages before you can begin writing. It is probably better to do them in the order shown here, but if that is difficult then do **2** then **1**.

1 **Refine the key message(s) of what you are trying to communicate.** This can take some time and if you find it difficult you can at least eliminate parts that are less important. For example, if you are analysing the disadvantages of an old computer system, then the exact technical details of the software are probably less significant than the fact that it has serious drawbacks, is out of date and no longer fulfils its original purpose.

   To work out what is your key message you also need to consider your document's audience and response. If you are writing a report for your Finance Director, for example, you will want to present the financial facts (e.g. cost, return on investment) as your key message. However, if your Finance Director has already given the go-ahead to installing the new system and you are writing a report for colleagues in Research and Development who will be using the system, then your approach will be different. Your key message may then be on the usability of the new system and its advantages compared with the old one.

2 **Organize the information.** In other words, you need to arrange the information you are giving in a certain order. The aim here is to find the most appropriate logical way to present what you want to say. Ways include:
   a arranging in terms of importance, probably listing the most important first
   b comparing the advantages and disadvantages
   c analysing different aspects of a scheme, e.g. under the headings political, legal, social, economic, financial
   d arranging in a chronological approach – considering a time sequence.

Writing the first draft

So you have prepared a pattern diagram and organized your thoughts in an appropriate order, and you now have come to the actual writing stage.

Now is the time to begin to write the following:

- an introduction to explain why you are writing your document
- the main part of your document, containing facts, explanations and other relevant information, together with your interpretation
- the conclusion: a summary of the key points, drawing together the issues you have raised.

Don't be tempted to ignore the preparation you have already done; build on that.

Let's now look at an example in the main part of your document. For example, you have on your pattern diagram the section:

old system
– keeps crashing
– secure?
– software: out of date
– slow, constant problems.

This is fine as a basis, but you need to expand these notes into sentences.

Let's say that this is a paragraph in your report. 'Old system' isn't adequate as a heading, so you write: 'Disadvantages of the existing system'. As you consider this subject, you realize that the key thought is 'The existing system, which was installed ten years ago, has been overtaken by many new technological features', so you put that as the opening sentence in your paragraph. (This is called 'the topic sentence' – one that represents the whole paragraph in a single sentence, showing what the paragraph is about.)

You can then fill out the rest of the paragraph, expanding on the note form of your original structure to express your meaning in sentences. If you are unsure what to write, keep asking yourself, 'What am I trying to say?' It can be very helpful to discuss this with another individual in person (not by email!) to sharpen up precisely what you want to communicate.

A first draft of the paragraph might read as follows. The raised numbers discuss certain aspects of the writing process. See end of passage for further explanation.

Disadvantages of the existing system

The existing system, which was installed ten years ago, has been overtaken by many new technological features. The present[1] system experiences too many failures[2], which cause colleagues a great deal of inconvenience[3]. Even when[4] the present system is functioning well[5], it is slow and often becomes locked[6]. Moreover[7], when handling large amounts of data, the existing system has been known to develop faults and some data has been lost. There are also doubts about how secure certain aspects of the system are.

Notes

1 To avoid repeating 'existing' I chose the synonym 'present'. Consult a thesaurus to help you with synonyms (words with similar meaning).
2 I thought that 'crash' was too informal for this report. I consulted a dictionary to help me find an alternative word.
3 I expanded on the effect of the computer failure.
4 'Even when' adds emphasis and a note of surprise considering the previous statement.
5 In my mind, I had 'running smoothly' but I felt that was too informal so I changed that to 'functioning well'.
6 In my mind, I thought of a computer 'freezing'; I thought that was too informal so consulted a dictionary and changed that to 'becomes locked'.
7 'Moreover' introduces a further similar line of reasoning; this additional thought occurred to me as I was writing, so I included it.

That is the first draft of one paragraph, with notes about why I wrote what I did.

Editing

After completing a draft, go back over it and refine it. The aim here is to ensure that what you have written is clear and as you want it. When I am editing a document, I check first what is there and second what is not there. Has the first draft missed out a vital step in the argument? Alternatively, you may find you have written too much about something that on further reflection was not very important and you have not written enough about something more important. Now is the time to redress that balance. Don't leave it as it is, thinking that it will go away or that the readers will not notice weaknesses in your argument.

Here are some tips for editing. Check that what you write:

- is accurate.
  - Check the content. We've all received emails inviting us to a meeting on Tuesday 14 September, only to discover that 14 September is a Wednesday. The result is that many colleagues spend precious time emailing requests for clarification and then having to respond to them with the exact date. It would have been better if the person who originally sent the message had checked the details before sending it.
  - Check totals of numbers, e.g. that percentages in a list all add up to 100.
  - Check punctuation. For example, are apostrophes and commas used correctly?
  - Check spellings. Be aware of words you often misspell. If your report contains basic errors, e.g. confusing *its* and *it's*, *effect* and *affect*, *of* and *off*, *principal* and *principle*, then they will undermine the overall credibility of your message.
- is brief. You may have heard of the saying, 'I wrote you a long letter because I didn't have time to write you a short one.' Sentences should be 15–20 words in length. If you put over 25 words, your readers may have difficulty following the meaning. Edit down – i.e. cut out – some parts of your text that do not add anything significant to your argument.

- is clear. Is your overall message clear? If it isn't to you, it will not be to your readers.
- contains appropriate language for the medium you are using.
  - Watch the tone of your writing. There is a tendency to be too informal in more formal contexts. For example, if you are describing the role of a project manager, you could say he/she needs to be able to 'keep many balls in the air', but such language would be inappropriate in a formal report, which might instead say 'tackle a wide range of activities at the same time'. There is also a tendency to be too formal, e.g. to use 'necessitate' instead of 'need', or 'terminate' instead of 'stop' or 'end'. The crucial point is to know who your audience is and write with them in mind.
  - There is a tendency these days to write using a sequence of nouns but a more effective way of communicating would be to use more verbs. For example, 'an examination of the maintenance records took place' would be better expressed as 'the maintenance records were examined' (passive) or, even better, 'the manager examined the maintenance records' (active, naming who examined the records).
  - Sometimes the language can be simplified: 'the repercussions regarding the effects subsequent to the

explosion will be perused by the staff' can be simplified to 'the managers will consider the effects of the explosion'.
- Avoid abbreviations that are not generally known and jargon and slang.
- follows a logical sequence of thought.
    - Often when you write a first draft, you tend to put down unrelated thoughts. At the editing stage, focus on each sentence to make sure it fits into a logical sequence of your thoughts. In the example above, I constantly used the phrases 'existing system' or 'present system' in the paragraphs to make sure the content of each sentence was clearly focused.
    - Similarly, the progression of your paragraphs should follow a logical thought: each paragraph or series of paragraphs should deal fully with one particular idea before you move on to the next idea or thought. You can sometimes use linking words and phrases to show the connection or contrast (e.g., to reinforce a point already made, *moreover, furthermore*; to introduce a contrast, *however, conversely, on the other hand*).
- expresses the meaning you want to communicate. Look back at the final sentence in my example: 'There are also doubts as to how secure certain aspects of the system are.' An alternative that rounds off the text better would be: 'Furthermore, faults in the present system have occasionally jeopardized (or *compromised*) the security of the overall network.'

Lists in bullet points

Consider whether the use of a list in bullet-point form is appropriate, especially for short phrases. People sometimes ask me about punctuation in bullet points: the trend these days is only to put a full stop at the end of the final point and not to have anything at the end of each point. If individual points consist of more than one sentence, think whether the list should be presented in bullet points.

A more frequent mistake is that individual lines do not run on grammatically from the opening text, e.g.:

> The successful candidate will be:
>
> ✔ skilled in numeracy and literacy
>
> ✔ able to speak at least two European languages
>
> ✗ have experience in using project-management software.
>
> The error here is in the third bullet point, which does not follow on grammatically from the opening line, and should be changed to:
>
> ✔ experienced in using project-management software.

I have deliberately gone into some depth at this editing stage to be very practical in what to write and how to express it.

All the above applies to extended documents; we can now turn to some specific kinds of document.

Writing emails

Emails are great. We can communicate with colleagues all round the world instantly. However, emails also have their disadvantages. We can receive too many unwanted ones that stop us dealing with the tasks we are supposed to be dealing with.

Here are a few tips:

- Put a clear subject in the subject line (more than 'Hi Jane'). Being specific about your subject will help your reader know what the email is about.
- Use 'cc' ('carbon copy', from the days of paper) and 'bcc' ('blind carbon copy') sparingly. Send copies only to those who really need to see the email. To explain 'cc' and 'bcc': if I am emailing Colin and cc Derek and bcc Ed, then Colin will see I have copied the email to Derek but Colin will not see I have copied the email to Ed. Using 'bcc' can also be useful for bulk emails when you don't want individuals to know the identity of the people on your emailing list.
- Unless you are writing to a close colleague, include some form of opening and closing greetings. The policy of your company and organization and your own personality will

guide you to what is acceptable (e.g. I find 'Hi Martin' difficult to accept from someone I don't know at all).

● In a long email, put the key information at the beginning, so that it will be clear on the opening screen as your reader opens the email. Spend some time laying out your email. Group sentences that concern one subject in paragraphs. Remember that, if your message isn't clear to you, then it certainly won't be clear to your readers!

● Watch the tone of your email to make sure it is not too abrupt. Consider adding softer opening and closing statements. Even 'Thank you' can help in this respect.

● Use only those abbreviations that are known to your readers.

● Don't type whole words in capital letters, which strongly suggest shouting.

● As part of your email 'signature', also include other contact information at the end of your email, including your job title, phone numbers (landline, mobile) and postal address. Your reader might want to phone you to clarify a point.

Writing letters

Although use of email is widespread, letters are useful for more formal statements. Business letters follow certain conventions:

● Opening greeting. If this is the first time you are writing to someone, use their title: Mr, Mrs, Ms, etc. If you know their first name, use that: 'Dear Freda'. You can also use the style of the person's first name and surname, especially if you are uncertain from the name (e.g. Sam, Jo, Chris) whether the recipient is male or female: 'Dear Sam Smith'. The style 'Dear Sir' or 'Dear Sir or Madam' is very formal and more impersonal.

● Closing greeting. If the opening greeting is 'Dear Freda', 'Dear Mrs Jones' or 'Dear Sam Smith', then the close is 'Yours sincerely' (capital 'Y' on 'Yours' and lower-case 's' on 'sincerely'). You can also add 'With best wishes' or 'Best wishes' before 'Yours sincerely'. If you have used 'Dear Sir' or 'Dear Sir or Madam' then the close is 'Yours faithfully' (capital 'Y' on 'Yours' and lower-case 'f' on 'faithfully').

Writing reports

The basics of writing reports

All the advice above on writing is important here, especially knowing why you are writing the report, who will be reading it and how you will structure it.

Kinds of report include:

- a progress report
- a health and safety report
- an investigation into the causes of an accident
- a company report
- a feasibility report
- a legal report used as evidence.

Your audience may be colleagues, shareholders, a board of directors, a project board, a team of advisers or consultants, a committee or users of a new product.

The purpose of your report may be to:

- examine whether a particular project, product, etc. is financially viable
- present a case for a decision on buying a product or service
- persuade someone to act in a certain way
- explain how a new product works
- describe the achievements, financial condition, etc. of a company
- inform colleagues of the progress of a project
- outline the cause of an accident or the nature of an incident.

Be clear about your audience, intention and response (see **Sunday**). Knowing these will determine, for example, how much information you should include in your reports. If in doubt, discuss with colleagues. In other words, do not agonize over writing ten pages when senior management want only one page. Moreover, your company or organization may already have a report template to give a structure to your report.

The content of reports

Reports normally have the following as a minimum:

- **Introduction**: this provides the report's purpose, including its scope or terms of reference.
- **Body of the report**: its main sections, outlining the procedure you have followed and findings, supported by facts and other information. Such objective evidence should be distinguished from your interpretation of those facts in your argument.
- **Conclusions**: a clear summary that draws all your arguments together, and recommends the necessary actions arising from your conclusions that must be taken to implement the report's findings.

Reports are often structured with clear numbers and headings (e.g. 1, 1.1, 1.1.1, 1.1.2, 1.2) to help readers refer to different parts easily.

Depending on the length of the report, you may also include:

- An executive summary of the whole report. Such a summary should be able to stand by itself and be a concise statement of all the report's significant information.
- Appendices: a section at the end of the report that contains technical information that is too long or too detailed to be included in the body of the text.
- Bibliography: a list of references and other sources of information used and/or quoted in the report.

Summary

Today we've looked at writing – first of all at the general principles that apply especially to longer documents:

- thinking
- organizing
- writing your first draft
- editing.

We then looked specifically at writing different kinds of documents: emails, letters and reports.

Exercise

1. Think which stage of writing you find most difficulty with (e.g. thinking, organizing, drafting, editing) and read again the relevant parts of today's chapter.
2. Look at an email that you have just received from a colleague. Is its message clear? Is its tone appropriate? Is the action your colleague wanted you to take clear?
3. Look at an email that you have just written. Is its message clear? Is its tone appropriate? Is the action that you want the reader to take clear?
4. What practical steps will you take to improve your emails?

SUNDAY

MONDAY

TUESDAY

WEDNESDAY

THURSDAY

FRIDAY

SATURDAY

Fact-check (answers at the back)

1. Is the idea 'I just start writing without any thinking or planning':
   a) good ❑
   b) bad ❑
   c) neither good nor bad ❑
   d) a waste of time? ❑

2. When writing in business, keep in mind:
   a) yourself ❑
   b) the weather ❑
   c) your readers ❑
   d) your boss. ❑

3. When I write a long document, I organize my material before I write:
   a) never ❑
   b) sometimes ❑
   c) why bother? ❑
   d) always. ❑

4. Getting the tone of an email right is:
   a) important ❑
   b) a luxury if you have the time ❑
   c) a waste of time ❑
   d) unnecessary. ❑

5. To help me write, I use a thesaurus or dictionary:
   a) never ❑
   b) what's a thesaurus? ❑
   c) very rarely ❑
   d) often. ❑

6. After you have drafted an email you should:
   a) press 'send' ❑
   b) go home ❑
   c) keep on rewriting it ❑
   d) check it. ❑

7. When re-checking an email before I send it:
   a) I never find anything I want to change ❑
   b) I'm a perfectionist, so I change so much that I forget to send it ❑
   c) I often change things ❑
   d) I don't bother to check them. ❑

8. When I send an email, I send a copy to:
   a) everyone in my address book ❑
   b) only those who need to see it ❑
   c) no one: I don't know how to do that ❑
   d) my boss always, to protect myself. ❑

9. When writing a report:
   a) I structure my material carefully ❑
   b) I don't bother structuring my material ❑
   c) I ask someone else to structure it ❑
   d) My structure is so elaborate even I don't understand it. ❑

10. When writing a report:
   a) I put all the material down, hoping that readers will be able to make sense of it ❑
   b) I carefully distinguish facts and interpretations ❑
   c) I put everything in lists of bullet points ❑
   d) I get so lost in writing that I don't really think about what I am writing. ❑

WEDNESDAY

Organize better meetings

Yesterday I met Tatiana. She started off in the company as an Assistant Editor. She had worked hard over the years and had now been promoted to Deputy Managing Director. She looked tired. I asked her if her life was full of meetings and she replied, 'Yes.' It was clear that many of the meetings she attended were too long and lacked focus and so had dampened her former enthusiasm.

A significant amount of your time as manager may be taken up in meetings, but they can go on too long and not achieve anything significant, and colleagues can become unenthusiastic or even cynical. How can you improve them?

Today we will look at:

- the purpose of meetings
- preparing for meetings
- chairing meetings
- participating in meetings and negotiating
- following up from meetings.

We will see that the key to a successful meeting lies in its preparation.

The purpose of meetings

Meetings are useful to:

● inform colleagues, e.g. to introduce new goals or give an update on progress
● discuss with colleagues, e.g. plan together the way ahead or evaluate a solution to a problem
● reach a decision and agree on the next steps to be taken.

Team meetings are also particularly useful to develop a sense of team identity as members interact with one another. As manager and team leader, you can use team meetings to encourage better teamwork and motivate your team (see also **Friday**).

'Time is money'

We sometimes say that 'time is money', but what does that mean? Suppose you earn £20,000 per year. If we divide this figure by the number of days you work productively, i.e. omitting holidays and allowing for illness, this could give, say, 46 weeks per year. £20,000 ÷ 46 = £434.78 per week or £86.96 per day, assuming five days per week. If we then divide this figure by the time per day you spend on productive work, say two-thirds of seven hours (= 4.66 hours), we come to £18.66 per hour: this is the amount that you are paid per hour gross, i.e. before tax and other deductions.

That is only half the story, however. Your actual cost to your company or organization is about twice that figure. This is to allow for overheads: the general business expenses, the taxes your company pays as an employer, the rent of an office building, heating, power, water, etc. So the cost to your company or organization is £18.66 × 2 = £37.32 per hour.

So, if a business meeting lasts seven hours and is attended by six colleagues, then the cost of that meeting to the company or organization is 7 × 6 × £37.32 = £1567.44, which is probably considerably more than you thought. It literally pays, then, to run a good meeting.

> The significance of this may help you decide how many people need attend your meetings and whether everyone needs to sit through the whole meeting or whether some colleagues need only come for the part that concerns them.

Preparing for meetings

TIP *The key to a successful meeting lies in the preparation.*

PLAN

The key to a successful meeting lies in the preparation. It is essential that you:

- **Know the purpose of the meeting.** Many meetings have no clear purpose and could easily be shortened or even cancelled. You need to be crystal clear about what you are trying to achieve.
- **Plan a venue and time** (start, finish) in advance. I've arrived at the stated venue for some meetings to find the meeting is in a different place.
- **Invite the key people** to participate in advance. If you want a director with a busy diary to be present, then it is no good inviting him or her the day before; you need to have invited them a long time before. It is also useful if you can discuss

with key people in private in advance any agenda items that could be controversial.

- **Circulate an agenda in advance.** This means that you will have thought about the structure and purpose of the meeting beforehand. Also, circulate important papers with the agenda, not at the meeting itself. Ideally, the length of such papers should be no more than one page each.
- **Prepare the meeting room.** Plan the seating: chairs around a table invite discussion; a chairperson at the end of a long table with ten seats either side, less so. If a PowerPoint presentation is being given, ensure a projector and connecting lead are set up. Check that the heating or air conditioning works.
- **Read reports in advance.** If reports have been circulated before a meeting, then read them. I have been in too many meetings where we have sat during the meeting reading material, which should have been undertaken in advance.
- **Ensure that you come up with accurate information.** For example, if the meeting is one to monitor progress, take all your latest data on progress with you.

Chairing meetings

The chair (chairman, chairwoman or chairperson) is the one who sets the tone for the meeting and guides the participants through the discussion. His/her tasks include:

- deciding the agenda in advance
- keeping to the agenda so that the meeting starts and finishes on time
- introducing and welcoming newcomers, or asking participants to introduce themselves
- reviewing progress on action points from previous meetings
- bringing in key individuals to contribute at appropriate points
- stating key aims and objectives
- summarizing progress of the points being discussed
- drawing together the points discussed, to reach agreement and draw conclusions and to make decisions; if a point has been controversial, the chair can express exactly what is to be minuted, to avoid possible misinterpretation later

- ensuring action points are clear, particularly who is responsible for following up particular points and by when. The action points should be SMART:
  - S: Specific, not vague, e.g. not 'We want to increase profits', but 'We want to increase profits by £100,000'
  - M: Measurable and quantifiable, e.g. with milestones along the way to assess progress
  - A: Agreed by all present at the meeting
  - R: Realistic or resourced, i.e. 'if you want me to complete this task, you need to provide me with the resources to enable me to do so'
  - T: Timed: when are actions to be completed by?
  Some colleagues also add -ER to give SMARTER:
  - E: Evaluated: at a later meeting, progress is assessed
  - R: Reported: the evaluation is recorded at a future meeting.

A good chair is a diplomatic and organized leader, someone whom the colleagues trust and someone who values, motivates and involves others, checking they understand the points discussed. Ideally, he/she will be able to quieten down those who talk too much and also draw out those who talk too little but can still make valuable contributions. A good chair will also sense when the time is right to bring a discussion to an end and be able to come to clear decisions.

Any committee is only as good as the most knowledgeable, determined and vigorous person on it. There must be somebody who provides the flame.

Claudia (Lady Bird) Johnson (1912–2007), widow of the former US president Lyndon B. Johnson

Rescuing a failing project

Imran was called in to troubleshoot on a failing project. The existing project manager was beginning not to cope with the growing responsibilities of the project. Fortunately, Imran had a good working relationship with him. Imran quickly noticed that basic points were missing: meetings were very poorly structured with the barest agenda; during the meetings, discussions rambled on for a long time, often without decisions being made; even when key action points were agreed, they were not noted, followed through or even ever reviewed at the next meeting. No wonder the project was in a mess! As Imran had good relationships with all the colleagues, he was quickly able to put in place well-structured meetings with good chairmanship, minute-taking, action points and reviews at the next meeting, so the project got back on track.

Good team meetings

Martha was a good team leader. The meetings she led were particularly good. She kept close to the agenda, which had been circulated before the meeting, and she followed up on the action points from the previous meeting. She prepared for the meetings well, thinking in advance how she might tackle objections to her ideas that colleagues might raise. She gave out overall information about how the company was performing and led fruitful discussions on how her unit could improve their efficiency even further. On confidential matters, she was diplomatic and as open as she could be. On difficult matters, she was able to identify the core issue and lead a discussion and evaluation of possible solutions before deciding on a particular course of action. She was particularly good at encouraging everyone to participate and express themselves. She always summarized the discussions and came to a clear decision about the next step. She made sure minutes of the meeting were circulated promptly after meetings so that colleagues were all clear about what they should do. The result was that colleagues in her team all felt inspired and well-motivated.

Participating in meetings

Everyone has a part to play in a successful meeting. I have never understood how people can come out of a meeting asking 'What was the point of that?' when they themselves have not contributed anything. Each of us has a role to play by:

- listening well and concentrating. Switch phones and other electronic gadgets off; avoid sending text messages; don't interrupt when someone else is talking.
- asking for clarification if you are unsure about a point that has been made. It is highly likely that other colleagues will also want clarification but have been afraid to ask, perhaps for fear of looking ignorant.
- being constructive: having a positive attitude. Even if you disagree with what has been said, there are positive ways of expressing a difference of opinion by challenging an idea without angrily criticizing the person expressing it or publicly blaming an individual for a wrong action.
- confronting issues. Focus on the real issues; don't get sidetracked. Too many of our meetings avoid discussing 'the elephant in the room', the subject everyone is aware of but doesn't mention because it is too uncomfortable.
- being willing to change your mind. If you are listening and persuasive arguments have been offered then allow yourself to be convinced by them and change your opinion about an issue.

Negotiating: win–win situations

In negotiating, we are aiming for a win–win situation. A win–win situation can perhaps be well illustrated by an example. My son Ben has just moved to Asia and he wanted to sell his camera. His friend Rob wanted a camera to take photographs on his travels. Ben sold Rob his camera – both won. Both gained what they wanted: Ben money, Rob a camera.

In his book *The 7 Habits of Highly Effective People*, Stephen R. Covey points out that the basis for a win–win situation is our character.

> *If you're high on courage and low on consideration, how will you think? Win–Lose. You'll be strong and ego-bound. You'll have the courage of your convictions, but you won't be very considerate of others. ... If you're high on consideration and low on courage, you'll think Lose–Win. You'll be so considerate of others' feelings that you won't have the courage to express your own. ... High courage and consideration are both essential to Win–Win. It's the balance of the two that is the mark of real maturity. If you have it, you can listen and you can empathically understand, but you can also courageously confront.*

The 7 Habits of Highly Effective People Personal Workbook, Stephen R. Covey (Simon & Schuster, 2005), p. 91

A good negotiator of contracts

Danielle was respected as a good negotiator in contracts. The secret of her success lay in good planning. She spent a long time thinking through different business models and pricing levels so that, when it came to the negotiations, she knew exactly what approach to take. After both sides had presented their initial case, she was sometimes able to detect the weak points in the arguments of the other side and exploit them according to her own personality. When they came to the final bargaining she had clarified the critical issue (the price) in her mind and knew the less significant matters she could be flexible on; she didn't mind bringing delivery of the products forward by six weeks. She was assertive and firm on what was non-negotiable, however: the price. So she was able to settle and close deals well and arrange the next steps in business relationships between the two sides.

Videoconferencing

Videoconferencing means that you avoid spending travel costs and that you can link colleagues over the Internet. Here are some tips to help you plan a videoconference session:

Make sure the room in which the meeting takes place has good acoustics and also is tidy.

Agree and circulate the agenda in advance to all participants. Appoint a chairman who can introduce the participants. Email any special presentations (e.g. PowerPoint) in advance.

Identify individuals using cards in front of them with their name on.

Remind participants to look at the camera while they are talking. Ask other participants to listen while one person is speaking.

Follow-up from meetings

A meeting where decisions are made but after which no one acts on these decisions is a waste of time. If colleagues have action points to pursue, those colleagues should follow them up.

The minutes of a meeting are a record of what happened in a meeting, including its action points. The person taking the minutes does not need to write down everything that goes on, but significant decisions, especially the action points concerning dates, schedules and financial matters, must be noted specifically.

The sooner the minutes of a meeting are circulated to those present at the meeting and other key colleagues, the more likely it is that colleagues will follow up the action points asked of them.

A good manager will also follow through between meetings on the progress of the key action items; he/she will not leave it to the next meeting only to discover that action has not been taken and so valuable time has been lost.

Summary

Today we've considered how to make your meetings more effective. I've particularly emphasized the need for careful preparation: think *why* you are holding the meeting (hopefully more than 'It's our normal monthly meeting'), *who* needs to be there, *what* you will consider, *when* it will start and finish and *where* it will take place. Plan and circulate the agenda in advance, together with any key documents. Make sure proper minutes are circulated promptly and then also reviewed at the next meeting, to ensure all the action points have been dealt with well.

Exercise

1 Think about a meeting that you have attended recently. What were its good points? What were its bad points? What practical steps can you take to ensure the bad points are not repeated in future?

2 If you are chairing meetings, what practical steps can you take to improve your leading of meetings?

3 If you are not chairing meetings, what practical steps can you take to improve your participation?

SUNDAY
MONDAY
TUESDAY
WEDNESDAY
THURSDAY
FRIDAY
SATURDAY

Fact-check (answers at the back)

1. My attitude to meetings is that:
a) occasionally they are productive ❏
b) they are boring ❏
c) they are a necessary evil ❏
d) I want to make sure they are better. ❏

2. The key to a successful meeting lies in the:
a) room ❏
b) participants ❏
c) length of time it lasts ❏
d) preparation. ❏

3. 'Every business meeting should have an agenda':
a) false ❏
b) true ❏
c) sometimes true ❏
d) if you say so. ❏

4. A good chairperson will:
a) summarize progress and make clear decisions ❏
b) wander away from the agenda ❏
c) let everyone have their say but never reach a decision ❏
d) expect all meetings to run smoothly. ❏

5. When a decision is made, ensuring someone is responsible for implementing that decision is:
a) nice to have ❏
b) a luxury ❏
c) essential ❏
d) we never make decisions. ❏

6. In setting SMART action points, the S stands for:
a) silly ❏
b) specific ❏
c) special ❏
d) standard. ❏

7. In setting SMART action points, the T stands for:
a) timed ❏
b) tough ❏
c) thought-through ❏
d) technical. ❏

8. If I'm not chairing the meeting:
a) I can send text messages to friends ❏
b) I can distract the colleagues sitting opposite ❏
c) I'm negative about my colleagues ❏
d) I know I still have an important part to play. ❏

9. If I'm in a meeting and don't understand what is being discussed:
a) I'm silent ❏
b) I want to go home ❏
c) I ask, even though it may make me look ignorant ❏
d) I wait for the chairman to explain it. ❏

10. After a meeting, minutes should be circulated:
a) what are 'minutes'? ❏
b) never ❏
c) promptly ❏
d) if we're lucky. ❏

THURSDAY

Give successful presentations

So far this week, we've looked at our aims, the importance of listening, writing documents and running better meetings. Today we come to another key aspect of your work as a manager that takes in all of the above: speaking, as you give a presentation.

You may never have given a presentation before and understandably you may be nervous, but you can relax, because the skills you need are the ones that you have been reading about and practising so far this week:

- know your aims – who you are speaking to; what you know about them (you gather that from listening); what your key messages are and what response you want from your audience
- plan what you want to say – you can build on the techniques you read about on Tuesday (for example, using a mind map to get your creativity going; planning and organizing)
- know your own special unique contribution to the meeting at which you are to speak.

So today we look at this, also discussing the use of visual aids, including PowerPoint, body language and feedback.

Lay a strong foundation

Look back at **Sunday** and AIR (Audience, Intention, Response). Who is your audience: senior managers? colleagues? colleagues from outside your company, some of whom might be critical?

How many will be in your audience: five, 50, 500? How much do they already know about what you are going to say? Will you need to sketch in some background? What are their thoughts and feelings towards you, as speaker, likely to be? Discover as much as you can about your audience before you plan your presentation.

Sometimes, when I give a presentation, I actually think of one or two real individuals in the audience and on the basis of my knowledge of them prepare as if I am speaking only to them.

Think why you are giving the presentation. What is the background context in which you have been asked to give it? Is there a hidden agenda?

Try to summarize your message in 12 words. For example, if I were speaking about the context of today's chapter in a presentation, the key message would be 'Prepare your presentation well'.

Remember practical points:

- Know how long you will speak for: 15 minutes? an hour? People will be grateful if you finish early (but not too early!) but will not appreciate it if you go on too long.
- Consider the layout of the seating. At one workshop I led with 15 delegates I complained that the suggested seating looked too much like that of a classroom, so we adjusted it to a 'horseshoe' or 'U' layout, which helped interaction between the participants. Don't forget the room's lighting, heating or air conditioning.
- Think about what you are going to say. Look back at **Tuesday** on using a mind map and answering the question words *why*, *how*, *what*, *who*, *when*, *where* and *how much*. You may think it unnecessary to do this but doing so is often fruitful, because you are putting down your key thoughts before you begin to organize and order them.

Before you organize your thoughts, I'm going to add an additional stage to the ones I gave on Tuesday. The key words in your mind map are probably nouns (names of things); the aim here is to add a verb (doing word) to make a more powerful combination. For example, a draft for this chapter was:

Foundation		Yourself
Message	Presentation	Body language
Visual aids		Feedback

I then added verbs to give:

Lay a foundation		**Prepare** yourself
Refine your message	**Give** a presentation	**Be aware of** body language
Prepare visual aids		**Expect** feedback

and I even went on to a third stage and began to add adjectives (describing words) to give:

Lay a **strong** foundation		Prepare yourself
Refine your message	Give an **effective** presentation	Be aware of body language
Prepare **useful** visual aids		Expect **positive and negative** feedback

Do you see? What I am trying to do is spread the load of the core meaning: rather than simply 'visual aids' I ended up with 'prepare useful visual aids'.

Use a thesaurus and/or a dictionary of collocations (word partners) to develop your words and phrases. Work on them, hone them, sculpture them so they clearly express what you want (*expect positive and negative* feedback; *refine* your message).

Organize your thoughts. You are now in a position to put your thoughts and basic messages in a certain order. You have worked out your key message 'Prepare your presentation well' and you can put the material in a certain order. Note that:

- you need to add an Introduction and a Conclusion; they are separate
- you should put your most important point first in the main part of your presentation.

The order of your draft may be different from the one you end up with. That is OK. It is only a draft. It is better to work on some order. For example I know that 'prepare useful visual aids' and 'expect feedback' are important but they are not the basic, primary aspects of what I am trying to say, so they can go later in the presentation. So the final order of my draft is as follows (you can compare this with the final text):

1 Lay a strong foundation		**6** Prepare yourself
2 Refine your message	Give an effective presentation	**4** Be aware of body language
3 Prepare useful visual aids		**5** Expect positive and negative feedback

In the end, I put '6 prepare yourself' as a short paragraph – not as a main point – under '4 be aware of body language'.

Refine your message

- Work out your key messages. Be crystal clear on what you are trying to say. Keep your 'headlines' simple. Don't try to cram too much in – 'less is more'.

- Break down your key points into subpoints. Work on your words. Use short everyday words rather than longer ones. So use *try* rather than *endeavour*; *need*, not *necessitate*; *stop* or *end* rather than *terminate*; *harmful* rather than *detrimental*.

- Say the same thing more than once. If your key point is 'Prepare well' then say that and add something like 'You need to work hard at the planning to make your presentation effective'. This is *expanding* on 'Prepare well', saying it again in different words. This is something you do more in speaking than in writing. You also do it in speaking when you see that your audience doesn't really understand what you are saying. This means you should look at them when you are speaking, not at your notes. Hopefully you are so familiar with what you want to say that you do not need to follow your script word for word.

- Think about how you will communicate. Ask questions. Give a specific case study (example) or tell a story to back up the point you are making. Include some well-chosen quotations or statistics. Be creative. Find a picture that will illustrate the key point of your talk (but make sure that you're not in breach of copyright if you use it).

- Work on different parts of your presentation. Work especially hard on the *beginning*, to capture your audience's attention with your introduction ('Did you know... ? I was reading in today's newspaper...') and the *end* ('So the next step is...') to round off your presentation, drawing together and reinforcing application of your key points.

- Structure your main points in a logical sequence. If you can structure them by making them all start with the same letter of the alphabet, or by 'ABC' (e.g. one of the talks I give on writing encourages writers to be *accurate, brief* and *concise*), then your points will be more memorable.

- Check your message. This is one of the key points for you to remember this week. Check facts and dates to make sure they are accurate.

- In your preparation, continue to think what the response of your audience is likely to be. Interested? Bored? In need of persuasion? Sceptical? Anticipate likely reactions by dealing with them in your preparation and preparing answers to questions.

- Write your presentation down. Either write down (1) every word you plan to say or (2) notes that you can follow. If you do (1), then don't read it out word for word from your paper. Hopefully, your thoughts will have become part of your way of thinking. As you gain more experience, you will probably find you can work from notes. When I started giving presentations I wrote everything in pencil (so I could rub words out), then I typed them up (and enlarged the printout so that I could read it). Now, with more experience, I write out the key points with important phrases or words highlighted. Do what you are comfortable with.
- Be enthusiastic; be positive. You have a message to declare. Go for it! Think about your own approach to your talk. You have your own unique personality, skills and experiences. Be natural; be yourself. It took me years to discover and work out my own style for giving presentations. I was amazed when a colleague contacted me after a space of five years to ask me to lead a workshop at his company and he said, 'I remember your style'.
- Plan in a break. If your presentation is going to last longer than 45 minutes, then schedule a break so that your audience can relax for a few minutes.

Unseen, but important preparation

Hasheeb was wise. He had given a few presentations and was beginning to enjoy them, even though he was always nervous before he gave one. He realized he would probably be giving presentations for a few years into the future, so he began to read more widely round the subject. He kept a hard-copy notebook and a computer file of useful ideas, stories, quotes and notes he came across. In this way, when he was asked to speak, he had a resource he could refer to, so that his interest and passion remained fresh. This unseen, but important, preparation work was one of the secrets of his effectiveness as a speaker.

Prepare useful visual aids

Will you give handouts of your presentation? How many will you need? Work out when you will give them out: before or at the end of the presentation? My personal preference is before, so that the audience knows where I am going. The disadvantage of that is that they do know where I am going, so always make sure that your notes are a skeleton (not the full text) of your presentation. Make enough copies of your handouts and some spare.

I made the mistake in one of my early presentations of preparing handouts that were in effect my full notes; so when a colleague said, 'We didn't really need to come, we could have just read your paper', I didn't have an answer.

Use tables and charts to support your points – but don't be so complex or technical that your audience can't understand what you are trying to say. Be as simple as you can be.

Use a flipchart if appropriate; I personally prefer a flipchart to a PowerPoint presentation as I find a flipchart more flexible than the rigidly ordered PowerPoint.

If you are using PowerPoint, then:

- Allow plenty of time to prepare the presentation, particularly if you are not familiar with the presentation software. To begin with, it is likely to take far longer than you think.
- Don't try to put too much information on the slides. Keep to your headings, not the complete outline of your talk.
- Keep to one main font. Use a large font, ideally at least 28 points. Aim to have no more than six lines per slide (do you remember peering over people's heads trying to read tiny print on a slide?). A sans serif font is easier to read than a serif one. Headings arranged left (not centre) are easier to read; capitals and lower-case letters are also easier to read than text in all capitals.
- Check the spelling of words on your slides.
- Work out which colours work well, e.g. red on grey, yellow on blue.
- Use tables and charts to support your message; bar charts, pie charts and flow charts that give the key information visually work well.

- Use illustrations that support your message, not ones that show off your (lack of!) design or animation skills.
- Don't put the key information at the bottom of slides; colleagues far away from the screen may not be able to see over other colleagues' heads.
- Rehearse the presentation with your notes/text in advance.
- Check whether you or a colleague will supply the projector, leads to connect the projector to your laptop and a screen. Arrive early to set everything up.
- Put your presentation on a memory stick (saved in earlier versions of PowerPoint for good measure) in case your laptop fails and you have to view it from someone else's laptop.
- Make sure that when you give your presentation your eye contact is with your audience, not with your laptop or the screen.
- Organize the room so that everyone can see the screen.

 Prepare your message so thoroughly that it becomes part of you.

A picture is worth a thousand words

Jason was looking for suitable illustrations to accompany a talk he was giving on encouragement. He was emphasizing the 'tough but tender' aspect of encouragement and had a picture of a father and son to illustrate tenderness. He found it more difficult to find one for the tough aspect, however, until he remembered one of the tableaux in the Bayeux Tapestry in which a Bishop Odo was said to 'comfort' his troops by prodding them with a club. In modern colloquial English he was 'giving them a kick up the backside' to goad them into action. The picture Jason found was a good illustration of the point he was trying to make.

Be aware of body language

A friend once told me, 'They are not listening to a message; they are listening to a messenger', so be yourself. Look smart and then you are more likely to feel smart and more confident. Dress professionally. A colleague and I once met a publisher to try and persuade them to take up the idea of a book we were working on. I was appalled when my colleague turned up in a sweatshirt and jeans – that wasn't the professional image I was trying to express!

When giving your presentation, stand up straight and relax your shoulders. Don't hide behind the lectern (although I'm aware that positioning yourself there can hide your nervousness); you could even move around the room a little.

Maintain good eye contact with your audience – for me that is the critical point. If you are using a flipchart or PowerPoint, don't look at that while you are speaking; look at your audience. But look across your whole audience, not just at those you like. Remember too that your whole posture will reveal a lot about yourself.

Use your voice well: speak sometimes loudly, sometimes softly; sometimes faster, sometimes more slowly. Don't mumble; speak out your words clearly. Be expressive: vary the tone in which you speak. Use hand gestures, according to your personality.

Smile (in my early days of giving presentations I went so far as to write the word 'Smile' on every page of my notes). Pauses can be useful to help your audience digest what you have just said.

Prepare your message so thoroughly that it becomes part of you. Practise it by speaking it out loud. This will also help you time it.

Prepare your *self* as well as your *message*. The important point here is to be positive: you have been asked to give a presentation, so others have confidence in you. Be as enthusiastic as possible. Control your nerves. Take deep breaths. Drink water.

In your actual presentation, be authentic. Sometimes at the beginning of the workshops I lead, when I sense that participants and I are all nervous, I will say, 'How are you feeling about today?', adding 'I'm as nervous as you.' Such genuine self-deprecating comments can help defuse their tension.

A difficult but good experience

Harry was keen to improve his presentation skills, so his colleagues recorded a presentation that Harry gave. Harry realized that watching himself on video was a difficult but useful experience. He noticed what mannerisms he was unaware of (jangling his keys), words he kept on repeating (his recurrent one was 'OK?'). But it was worth it. The awkwardness and embarrassment he felt were a necessary part of his own learning experience. Becoming aware of his faults as others saw them was an important first step to his correcting them, as part of fulfilling his overall desire to become an even more effective presenter.

Expect positive and negative feedback

'Feedback' means questions from your audience – and you would be wise to prepare for them. These days I think a trend is to say at the beginning of a talk something like, 'I'll take any questions for clarification during the talk but please keep any more significant questions to the end.' If you say that, allow time, both for questions to aid your audience's understanding during the talk but also for the more significant questions at the end.

Here, as with so much of what you have read this week, the key lies in good preparation. Expect feedback. Expect a particular colleague to raise objections because that's what he/she always does. Expect them – and plan for them. Deal with their objections, and where possible return to the key messages you want to communicate. (I learned a trick here: when replying to an objector, don't keep eye contact only with that person, but let your eyes roam more widely through the room. If, while you give your answer, you look only at the person raising the objection, then he/she may take that as an opportunity to respond even further.)

If you don't know the answer to a question, be honest enough to say so. Often other colleagues in the room may be able to help you out. Conclude a question and answer session by again positively highlighting the key message(s) you want to communicate to round off the whole presentation.

After your presentation, evaluate it. You could also ask trusted colleagues to give their realistic assessment of your performance. What was the content like? Was your delivery/ presentation too slow or too fast? Was it directed at the right level? Did the handouts/visual aids/PowerPoint detract from or add to your presentation? Recognize what worked well but don't be afraid to acknowledge what didn't work so well, so that you can learn lessons for the future. Remember, 'the person who never made mistakes never made anything'.

Summary

Today we've looked at giving presentations. We've seen that to give an effective presentation means that you need to prepare well. You will:

- know who you are speaking to
- know what you are trying to achieve by your talk
- think about what you want to communicate
- plan and organize your thoughts
- work hard at the logical order and structure of your presentation
- work hard at your words
- work hard at your introduction and conclusion
- prepare any visual aids or PowerPoints but be as simple as possible; don't try to be too clever
- be aware of your body language as you deliver your talk. Be especially aware of keeping good eye contact with your whole audience.

Exercise

Think about a presentation you have to give in the next few weeks. Write out your key message in 12 words.

SUNDAY
MONDAY
TUESDAY
WEDNESDAY
THURSDAY
FRIDAY
SATURDAY

Fact-check (answers at the back)

1. You've got to give a presentation in a week's time. Do you:
   a) prepare well? ❏
   b) panic? ❏
   c) get so nervous that you don't prepare at all? ❏
   d) not bother preparing, knowing you are good at improvising? ❏

2. What is the most important aspect about giving a presentation?
   a) working out what PowerPoint slides you can use ❏
   b) knowing how long you are to speak ❏
   c) knowing what the weather is like ❏
   d) knowing what your key message is. ❏

3. When preparing what I am going to say:
   a) I jot down the first thing that comes into my mind ❏
   b) I take it slowly, thinking about my key message ❏
   c) I don't prepare; I just improvise on the day ❏
   d) I spend all my time thinking but never writing anything. ❏

4. When giving a presentation, repeating what you say using different words is:
   a) useless repetition ❏
   b) useful to reinforce your message ❏
   c) nice if you have a thesaurus ❏
   d) a waste of time. ❏

5. When constructing my argument:
   a) I carefully order the points I want to make ❏
   b) I don't bother organizing my points ❏
   c) I improvise ❏
   d) I lose the train of thought in my whole talk. ❏

6. When I think about my conclusion:
   a) I just repeat my six main points ❏
   b) conclusion – what's that? ❏
   c) I round off my presentation with the next steps I want my audience to take ❏
   d) I add two new points to liven up my talk. ❏

7. I use PowerPoint:
   a) always, as I want to show off my technical skills ❏
   b) never; I hate technology ❏
   c) usually, and put nearly all of my presentation on it ❏
   d) wisely, to support the points I want to make. ❏

8. When giving my presentation:
   a) I keep my eyes on my notes ❏
   b) I look only at my colleagues ❏
   c) I look at the pretty girls in the room ❏
   d) I look around widely at the audience. ❏

9. When speaking:
a) I vary the speed and volume of what I say ☐
b) I always speak in one tone ☐
c) I think I'm as bored as my audience ☐
d) I often use such words as *um* and *just*. ☐

10. I expect feedback from my presentation:
a) rarely ☐
b) never ☐
c) often ☐
d) if I am lucky. ☐

FRIDAY

Build strong working relationships

In a book on business communication, you could assume that it would all be about finding the right formula to include in an email and choosing your words carefully in a presentation, but there is something underlying and deeper going on: developing good working relationships. Good working relationships are the glue that holds a company or organization together.

We can also express that positive idea negatively: bad working relationships – or the absence of good (or any) working relationships – will mean that the company or organization will not function well.

I chose the words in the title of this chapter very carefully. *Build*: we can take active steps to cultivate and work at relationships; *strong* working relationships are ones that are firmly established – which takes time – and are not easily broken.

So today we consider how we can cultivate such strong working relationships, and how they are seen in practice, including working in teams, in delegating work and in resolving conflict.

Develop better working relationships

 TIP *Good working relationships are the glue that holds an organization together.*

I want this chapter to be practical. Establishing good rapport – a sense of mutual respect, trust and understanding – seems to come naturally and easily to some people, but not to others. My wife is much more naturally confident with people than I am, but she has taught me some skills that have helped me.

Here are some tips. I hesitate to call them 'techniques' because that can make them seem artificial and, if you try them, that could make them appear awkward.

- See things from another person's point of view. Listen to them – really listen to them (look back at **Monday** for more hints on listening).
- Pay attention; be genuinely interested in other people. I hesitate to write 'look interested' because that is all it could be – an appearance without a genuine interest. Smile; look at them; make eye contact with them.

- Notice colleagues' body language. Do you sense they are awkward or relaxed? What expression do they have on their face? Does their tone of voice reveal their insecurity? However, be aware that you can misinterpret people's body language. A speaker was giving a talk and a colleague in the audience had her eyes closed. The speaker interpreted the closed eyes as a sign of lack of interest whereas in fact they helped the colleague concentrate on the speaker's message.
- Adapt what you want to say to colleagues to suit them. This, for me, is vital. For example, when I lead a two-day course on communications I am aware that the time before the mid-morning break on the first day will be spent mainly *listening* to the participants – e.g. how they are fed up with the politics of their company; how their bosses do not listen to them or value them. Once these colleagues have got these feelings off their chest, they are ready to listen to what I have to say. If I were to start off with great enthusiasm and energy with *my* presentation and ignore the context of their frustration, they would not be ready to listen to me. I have to 'get onto their wavelength' – understand them first – and then adapt what I want to say to the reality of their situation as I have discovered it to be. In fact, I often explicitly say at the beginning of my courses, 'I am more interested in helping you than in getting through my material.'
- Be flexible in your response. If you are truly focused on the person you are talking to rather than on yourself, you will have a variety of responses available to you, e.g. 'One solution to this is...', 'Only you can decide' or even 'I'm not sure we're answering the right question. Isn't it more about...?'
- Notice what colleagues are saying. Pick up on their key thoughts and words. For example, I recall a meeting some years ago to discuss different departments' allocations of income in their budget. One head of department said he was 'firing a warning shot across the bows', that he was prepared to strongly oppose any attempts to reduce his department's budget. Knowing looks were exchanged by other colleagues and the chair of the meeting immediately withdrew his suggestion that his colleague's department should suffer a reduction in funding.
- Engage in 'small talk', conversation about ordinary things that are relatively unimportant from a strictly business point

of view. When you meet someone for the first time, it's all right to talk about their travel to the venue, the weather, their family, the previous night's football results, holiday plans, etc. Engaging in such conversation helps the actual business run more smoothly than if you did not have such conversation. Share a little of how you see life; ask questions, especially closed questions (ones that can be answered with a straight 'yes' or 'no') to begin with and then move onto some open questions (ones that may begin with *why, how, who, when, where, what* and get people talking), but don't make it seem as if you are interrogating the other person.

- Be aware of roles. When you meet someone for the first time and they tell you they are, for example, a dentist, doctor, police officer or accountant, be aware that you will probably then put them into a category of that profession and that you will trust them accordingly. On more on roles within a team, see later today.
- Be aware of colleagues' status and power, but treat each person as a unique individual. If you meet a headteacher for the first time, you may assume he or she has a lot of authority and you may feel insecure because you have a lower status than they do. However, the problem may be more in your perception than in reality. If the headteacher genuinely says to you, 'I'm interested in what you can tell me about...', you may feel honoured that a person in such a position of authority has asked for your opinion. For me, what is important is valuing each person as unique. I recall a comment on a teacher friend years ago: 'He even talks to the cleaners.' Realize that you can crush someone's sense of identity by belittling them, constantly interrupting them or ignoring them. Treat each person as a unique individual.
- Communicate what you are doing clearly and consistently and also why you are doing it. This is particularly important in introducing change management; you will constantly need to state why you are doing things to counter the 'we've always done it this way' approach.
- Ensure, as far as it is up to you, that the messages expressed by different departments in your company or organization are consistent, i.e. that they don't contradict one another.

- Put the aims of your company or organization first and make sure you fulfil your own work to the best of your capabilities. In most organizations there will be office politics and you will find people you like and people you don't like. Part of doing your job professionally is rising above, as far as you can, any different outlooks that colleagues have and their diverse personalities. Always be polite; don't engage in gossip. You may need to stop complaining about your colleagues and make sure you do your own work as professionally as possible.

Introducing changes gradually

Martha was promoted to team leader and had many good ideas on changing things, for example by introducing team statistics, rotas, new personal targets. However, her colleagues reacted badly to the speed of changes and her mentor had a quiet word with her ('Go for "evolution", not "revolution"').

So Martha slowed down and introduced the changes at a more measured pace, explaining to each colleague in informal one-to-ones why changes were necessary. The result was that her colleagues felt more valued and their self-confidence increased as they successfully navigated the changes.

A close working relationship

I've worked with Tony for over 30 years. We've worked on many long-term projects together: he as designer, I as writer/editor. We trust and respect one another for our different skills and experience. We've talked things through when we have had opposing views, to reach a positive solution. I phone him regularly when he is slightly behind schedule. We ask each other's opinion when we are unsure how to proceed. In 2011 we were awarded a prize for the work we and others had undertaken on *Collins Bible Companion* in a 'Reference Book of the Year' competition. When other colleagues have joined us in meetings, they have noted how we tend to think each other's thoughts and express them. Over our long period of collaboration, we have built up a close working relationship.

Develop stronger teamwork

A team is a group of diverse people who are working together towards a common goal. Team members bring a wide range of roles, which should *complement one another*: one person's weakness is balanced out by another person's strengths.

How can you build stronger working relationships in a team? One way is to be aware of different roles. A widely known set of roles was developed by Dr Meredith Belbin as he looked at how team members behaved. He distinguishes nine different team roles:

- **plant**: creative, good at coming up with fresh ideas and solving difficult problems in unconventional ways
- **resource investigator**: outgoing; good at communicating with outside agencies
- **co-ordinator**: good as chairperson, focusing team members on the goals; a good delegator
- **shaper**: dynamic action person who can drive a project forward through difficulties
- **monitor/evaluator**: able to stand back and bring objective discernment
- **team worker**: bringing harmony and diplomacy for good team spirit
- **implementer**: dependable, efficient practical organizer
- **completer/finisher**: able meticulously to follow through on details to complete a project
- **specialist**: giving expert technical knowledge.

For further details and how to identify colleagues' different roles, see www.belbin.com.

This analysis is useful since it can reveal possible gaps, i.e. your team may be lacking certain skills, which you can then seek to cover. For example, discussing these roles on one committee I was part of revealed we had no monitor/evaluator, someone who could stand back and objectively assess ideas. Identifying someone with those skills was therefore one of our aims.

Encourage better teamwork

As team leader, you are responsible for encouraging your team to work together successfully. To do that, you need to:

- Communicate a vision. Where is the team going? What is its purpose? As leader, you need to present a strong and inspiring vision of your goals.
- Set your goals clearly. There is nothing like an abstract statement which is not earthed in reality to turn people off. It is hardly surprising that colleagues come out of a team meeting feeling cynical when only a vision has been cast but no practical implications have been drawn from that vision. A vision must be turned into practical steps.
- Ensure your team values are agreed. Do team members trust and respect one another? Do individuals feel important and part of something bigger than themselves? Encourage team members to remain positive, to believe in the strength and unity of the team.
- Clarify responsibilities of each member of the team so that not only each individual knows their responsibilities but also the whole team knows what each member does. Different members of the team will bring different skills, so play to colleagues' strengths. For example, don't give the chairmanship of a meeting to someone who is unclear or indecisive.
- Ensure lines of authority and responsibility are clear. Be clear about whether individual team members have authority to spend sums of money up to a certain amount or should direct all requests for purchases through you as team leader.
- Show that you value team members. Listen to them; provide opportunities for members of your team to approach you if they need help. You should not be aloof; be available for them to bring their concerns to you. Understand them. Try to find out 'what makes them tick'. Talk to them (not *at* them). Find out what interests them outside work.
- Show that you value their work. One worker worked in a factory for years producing a small part in a large machine without knowing what the large machine was for. He was amazed,

and felt more fulfilled, when he knew the function of the large machine and where his work fitted into the overall picture.

- Ensure their work is interesting and challenging. No one likes boring repetitive tasks. Make sure your colleagues' work contains at least some interesting tasks that will stretch them.
- Be flexible about what is negotiable and different styles of working. Listen to suggestions from your colleagues. Be prepared to 'think outside the box' to find solutions to difficulties.
- Be fair and treat all your colleagues equally, even though you may like some more than others.
- Make sure all team members work as hard as each other; everyone has to 'pull their weight'. You can't afford to carry 'passengers': those team members who work significantly less than others.
- Show enthusiasm in your work. Enthusiasm is infectious, and so is the lack of it. If you are half-hearted in your commitment, that will show in your tone of voice and body language, and colleagues will be aware that you may be saying all the right words but not believing them yourself.
- Encourage openness. As far as you can, involve members of the team in making decisions. Bring out those who are shy and use your skills of diplomacy to quieten those who talk too much.
- Encourage team members to use their initiative. They do not always need to come back to you to solve small difficulties but can be enterprising and resolve issues themselves.
- Encourage colleagues to look out for one another, so that, for example, when one colleague is struggling, a fellow team member can step in and help.
- Encourage uncooperative colleagues to try a new system if they are reluctant to follow it, or even ask them if they could suggest new ways of solving a problem.
- Focus on specific, measurable, agreed, realistic/resourced and timed goals (look back at **Wednesday** for SMART goals), not on vague ideas.
- Give feedback. You as team leader should give informal feedback to team members on whether they are doing well ... or not so well. Be specific (e.g. 'I thought the tone of your email in response to the complaint was excellent') as far as possible.

Back to the shop floor

As Managing Director, Joe felt he needed to 'get back to the shop floor' and find out what his staff really thought of his organization. So he sat alongside members of staff for several days, listening to their concerns. They didn't feel their work was valued, and communications from 'them' (senior management) were thought to be very poor. At the end of the week, Joe was able to take these valuable lessons back to his role as MD and begin to change the company's practices.

Delegate well

Delegate more rather than less. There are a few matters you cannot delegate (e.g. managing the overall team, allocating financial resources, dealing with confidential matters of performance management and promotion), but you can and should both delegate many of your actual work tasks and some routine admin activities. Here are some further guidelines for good delegation:

- Be clear about the tasks you want to delegate. Don't give vague instructions (e.g. 'Could you write a short report on failings in security?') but be specific: 'I'd like a ten-page report giving examples of major security breaches together with possible reasons behind them and recommendations on how to avoid them in future.'
- Check that the person has understood the task you want him/her to undertake. Do this not by just asking, 'Have you understood what I want you to do?' but something like 'Could you summarize what you will be doing?' Their response will show how much they have understood your explanation.
- Give background details, so that the colleague knows why he/she is doing the task and how his/her task or activity fits into the overall scheme of things.
- Where necessary, follow up any spoken instructions in writing with a full brief, outlining the work.

- State the time by which you want your colleagues to complete the work. Remember that what may take you (with all your experience) a short time will probably take much longer for the colleague you are delegating to.
- Supervise their work properly: provide the necessary equipment and other resources that the colleague needs.
- Let the person to whom you are delegating the work decide the details of how he/she will undertake the work.
- Where problems arise, encourage the person to whom you are delegating to come to you not only with the difficulty, but also with thoughts on possible solutions.
- When your colleague has completed the task, thank the person, expressing your appreciation. Recognize him/her and the achievement.

Learning to trust

Oliver was usually fine at delegating tasks. He explained tasks well and let his team members get on with it, checking both informally – 'How's it going?'– as well as, less often, formally. However, with one colleague, Janet, he used to continually come and stand by her desk, moving about nervously, and constantly ask how she was getting on. This annoyed Janet so much that one day she lost her temper with Oliver and burst out, 'Why don't you trust me just to get on with the job?' Oliver had to learn to back off and gradually was able to trust Janet, enabling her to continue her work with less supervision.

A good salesman

Andy was a good salesman. Over the years, he had networked widely, earning his clients' trust and the right to be listened to ... and to sell his products. He was known for his commitment, thoroughness and integrity.

He was also persuasive. He was an astute listener, empathizing with and respecting his clients, and so was aware

> of their needs, helping his customers to make an informed choice. He was able to match his products to his clients' requirements because he genuinely wanted to provide products that were of real value to them. He knew his subject well and was very passionate about it. He really did believe in his products. So no wonder he was the country's best salesman.

Resolve conflict

At times you are bound to meet conflict. Trust breaks down. Personalities clash. Departments each want a bigger slice of the budget or to avoid the biggest cutbacks.

Deal with conflict quickly; tackle the issues. Don't be cautious and fearful about speaking directly and clearly about difficulties.

I've found the books *Difficult Conversations: How to Discuss What Matters Most* by Douglas Stone, Bruce Patton and Sheila Heen (Michael Joseph, 1999) and *The Peacemaker: A Biblical Guide to Resolving Personal Conflict* by Ken Sande (Baker, 1991) very useful. The following is based on what those authors helpfully suggest:

● Distinguish the incident – what is happening/happened – from feelings about the incident. Consider separately:
  – the incident – someone said something; someone is to blame. Try to focus on the real issue. Remain calm. Listen closely. Ask open questions. Understand other people's interests as well as your own.
  – feelings about the incident, e.g. anger, hurt
  – the identity of the person. Sometimes a person's identity, including their own self-worth, will feel threatened. Calmly affirm your respect for them.
● Do what you can to resolve the issue and maintain the relationship if possible: prepare and evaluate possible solutions to agree on the way forward.

Summary

Today we have been concerned with cultivating stronger working relationships: establishing a better rapport between colleagues. Key to this is taking the time to understand your colleagues and develop even greater respect and trust and stronger teamwork.

Exercise

1 Think about the colleagues in your company or organization. Think about the ones you like. Why do you enjoy working with them? Now think about the ones you don't get on so well with. What practical steps can you take to improve your working relationships with them?

2 Think about what you can do to rise above the petty aspects of office politics. What can you do (and what can you not do) to be even more professional in your work?

3 Think about an area of conflict at work. What can you do to listen to people's different viewpoints and distinguish the incident from feelings about the incident? What are the next steps for you to undertake?

SUNDAY

MONDAY

TUESDAY

WEDNESDAY

THURSDAY

FRIDAY

SATURDAY

Fact-check (answers at the back)

1. Having strong working relationships in an organization is:
   a) a luxury ❏
   b) essential ❏
   c) a waste of time ❏
   d) unimportant. ❏

2. In trying to build better relationships, think more about:
   a) yourself ❏
   b) your boss ❏
   c) your colleagues ❏
   d) your holidays. ❏

3. When you are in a discussion with colleagues:
   a) make sure you say what you have to, not thinking about your colleagues ❏
   b) look at your notes and never make eye contact with them ❏
   c) be embarrassed because you like them a lot ❏
   d) listen and respond to what they are saying. ❏

4. I'm aware of colleagues' body language, posture and tone of voice:
   a) never ❏
   b) always ❏
   c) rarely ❏
   d) often. ❏

5. 'Small talk' is:
   a) a useful tool to establish rapport ❏
   b) a complete waste of time ❏
   c) more important than the actual business ❏
   d) just about adequate. ❏

6. When thinking about others' roles:
   a) I am awed by those with higher status ❏
   b) I am very bossy towards those with lower status ❏
   c) I have this at the back of my mind but don't let it control me ❏
   d) I don't think about others. ❏

7. In our team, we are clear about having:
   a) strictly defined roles that we discuss whenever we meet ❏
   b) different roles that we use as a basis to help us ❏
   c) no set roles at all ❏
   d) all the same roles. ❏

8. I'd like to improve teamwork in my team:
   a) but it's already as good as it can be; I don't need to do anything more ❏
   b) and I'm keen to take practical action to do so ❏
   c) but I'm so aware of my failings as team leader ❏
   d) but I'm too lazy to do anything about it. ❏

9. When I delegate work, I do so:
   a) clearly ❏
   b) never. What is delegation? ❏
   c) in a vague way, hoping the colleague will work out what I mean ❏
   d) in so much detail that I confuse everyone. ❏

10. When resolving conflict, first of all I:
a) go straight to the solution ☐
b) put off dealing with it ☐
c) ignore everyone ☐
d) listen closely to what both
   sides have to say. ☐

SUNDAY

MONDAY

TUESDAY

WEDNESDAY

THURSDAY

FRIDAY

SATURDAY

SATURDAY

Engage effectively online

We conclude our week by looking at how you can develop an online presence and engage in business online, from the point of view of communication. Much of what we discuss today builds on what you have read earlier this week: this chapter pulls together a number of themes that we have already discussed, such as writing with a particular audience in mind, writing clearly and developing effective business relationships.

Websites have become an essential part of business life and it is difficult to imagine how we ever managed without them. Yet we are also aware that some websites are easier to navigate than others and information is more accessible on some than on others. So today we will consider:

- knowing your aims and planning your website carefully, so that the information is organized in a way that is accessible to the users you want to target
- writing text for your website, with tips on design and layout of your words
- exploiting the importance of social media in business.

Your company website

Know your aims

As I have mentioned several times throughout this week, it is essential that you clarify the exact aims of your website.

You may say that your company's or organization's website is your 'shop window', but what exactly do you mean by that? Your website will show the location of your office or store, and your opening hours. The website may show your goods or services, but do you want customers to buy direct from you or through a retailer or other intermediary? How do you want interested users of your website to respond to you? If you are offering a service, and if users want to complain, do you want to make it easy or more difficult for them to do so? You may want to promote an author or a rock band. You may want to inspire users by your choice of photographs, stories or poems. You may want to inform or educate users about a particular need or hobby and maybe ask them to give money towards your cause.

Plan your website

Work out your users' needs. We're back to AIR (Audience; Intention; Response), which we looked at on **Sunday**.

What are your users' needs? To know the aims of your company or organization? To be persuaded that they need to buy your product or service or ought to donate money? One way of beginning to think about this is to write a brief mission statement. You can fill this out with longer explanatory paragraphs and case studies (real-life examples) of your company or organization at work.

Think hard about how and when your users will use your website and what information they want. For example, we are currently renovating our bathroom and have accessed different companies' websites for details of the tiles, baths, basins, etc. they offer. Some companies give prices on the website, some in a separate downloadable brochure; some don't give prices at all!

Some users will view your website for only a few moments; others want to read what you have to say and respond positively, for example by buying a product or finding the information they want. Do you want users to download further files (e.g. in PDF)? How do you want users to contact you? Think it through practically and realistically.

Organize your website

Here are some tips:

- Plan a hierarchy of information, i.e. how you want users to go from one page to the next.
- Remember that people will navigate your site in a variety of ways.
- Separate your information into major – but manageable – parts. Group such parts into categories.
- Plan from 'the bottom up'; start with your most detailed pages and work backwards to your home page.
- Allow for flexibility. For example, if you are selling ebooks in various formats, allow for further tabs on your website alongside your existing ones to anticipate future changes in technology.
- Imagine a user accessing your website and work through how he/she will navigate your site. Make sure that the choices you are offering are the ones you want to offer. Some websites are built on the 'three-click' principle: give users the information they want within three clicks from the home page or they will go elsewhere. But the truth is, in reality, if users are interested – and determined – enough, they will explore your website more deeply.

- Have a balanced combination of words and images. Some websites seem to contain only words; some only images. I think an effective website will contain both (look back at **Sunday**).
- Plan how you will maintain your website. It is fine to work very hard on your website now, making it live by a certain date, but you also need to plan how you will keep it up to date. Too many websites have a section with 'latest news' that give stories that happened a year ago or more. Having out-of-date information does not communicate an image that your company or organization is successful now. So the rule is: plan to keep your website fresh.
- Consider specifically search engine optimization (SEO): how you will reach your target audience most effectively through the use of keywords, tags, etc.

A new concept

Ray, one of the directors of the plumbers Smithson and Son, asked Jo, a website consultant, to design and build their company's website. When Jo first met Ray, she explained that a website was different from the normal printed pages of a book, in that a website does not really have a finishing point; it is much more flexible than the traditional printed page. Pages are more like photographs: they provide a visual snapshot for users. This interactive nature of the website was an entirely new concept to Ray. Previously, he thought he could just put his company's existing leaflets on the website and that was it. Jo helped Ray see that the company's website could open up a whole new world, enabling customers to see what the company offered.

Write your website

Here are some useful tips:

- Keep in mind your users' needs. You are writing for them, not for yourself. Writing for a website is like having a conversation, except you cannot see the person you are talking to.

- Make sure your home page says:
  - who you are and your basic aims
  - the goods and/or services you offer
  - how users may obtain your goods and/or services.
- Make your text easy to read. Good practice has shown:
  - not to put text right across the whole width of the screen; if you do so, the text will not be legible. It is better to use up to half the width of the screen
  - the best position is towards the top of the screen and towards the left
  - text that is centred on the page is difficult to read, so align your text – including headings – to the left, but keep the right-hand side 'ragged' (unjustified)
  - a sans serif font is more legible than a serif one on a computer screen
  - you should keep the colours of your text and background different, but don't use too many colours.
- Give each page its own title.
- Divide your text into paragraphs and write a clear heading above the paragraph. Keep paragraphs to no more than 100 words.
- Have white space around your text; this creates an impression of openness.
- Put the most important information first in each paragraph.
- Use everyday words that you would say in a normal conversation, e.g. *explain*, not *elucidate*; *more* or *extra*, not *supplementary*.

- Keep your sentences short: a maximum of 15–20 words.
- Make sure your text is clear. Draft the text and then revise it, asking yourself what the paragraph is about. For example, some friends were writing about fishing for their website but had assumed that their readers knew all about that particular kind of fishing. When we discussed this, it became clear that what was missing was an opening definition of the particular kind of fishing they were writing about.
- Add hyperlinks to other pages on your website and/or back to your home page, e.g. Click here to find out more or contact us. (When users click on the underlined words they will be taken to a new page or a form.) Excessive use of hyperlinks can, however, make the page look too detailed.
- Make sure your spelling is correct. 'Stephenson' or 'Stevenson'? 'Philips' or 'Phillips'? Be consistent (e.g. use -*ise* or -*ize* throughout).
- Keep punctuation to a minimum; full stops at the ends of bullet points can make a website look fussy.
- Avoid abbreviations that are not generally known and jargon and slang.
- Put information in lists, which work well on websites.
- Make sure your text is accurate. Check dates and financial information so that they are correct.
- Look back at editing documents on **Tuesday** for further guidelines.

Business and social media

In recent years, as the pace of innovation in the Internet age has quickened, use of social media sites such as Facebook has become an important part of many people's lives. The impact of these sites is still being assessed but undoubtedly digital formats will remain immensely significant for the foreseeable future.

- Professional networking sites such as LinkedIn allow you to keep informed about trends in your area of business, network with colleagues around the world, discuss matters of common interest and see what business opportunities may arise.

● Blogs and Twitter help you to develop an online community by connecting with potential and existing clients, sharing links to interesting articles, exchanging pictures, information and specific insights, discussing ideas and asking – and responding to – questions.

Summary

Today we've looked at engaging effectively online by first of all considering your website: how to know your aims and move on from those to planning and organizing your website so that it fulfils those aims. We then looked at different aspects of writing for your website to make sure your message is communicated successfully.

As an effective manager, you will also want to engage with your potential and existing customers using online social media. It can be very useful to think which online media networks will be most profitable both in the short term (spreading the message now) and also in the medium and long terms (maintaining good business relationships).

Exercise

1 Summarize the aim of your website in 12 words.
2 Now think about your website and think how much it fulfils that aim.
3 How will you change and maintain your website to make sure it stays up to date?
4 How effective to your business are the social media sites that you use?

SUNDAY
MONDAY
TUESDAY
WEDNESDAY
THURSDAY
FRIDAY
SATURDAY

Fact-check (answers at the back)

1. Your website is:
   a) a luxury ☐
   b) a waste of time and money ☐
   c) essential ☐
   d) nice to have when you can afford it. ☐

2. Your website is your organization's:
   a) shop window ☐
   b) rubbish tip ☐
   c) set of printed leaflets ☐
   d) IT department's responsibility. ☐

3. The first thing to do when planning a website is:
   a) start writing as soon as possible ☐
   b) organize the pages ☐
   c) be flexible ☐
   d) know your aims. ☐

4. When designing web pages, put text in:
   a) whatever the committee we'll set up decides ☐
   b) less than half the width of the screen ☐
   c) the whole width of the screen ☐
   d) more than the width of the screen. ☐

5. Working out how users will navigate the website is:
   a) a luxury ☐
   b) essential ☐
   c) a waste of time ☐
   d) important if you have the money. ☐

6. When designing web pages:
   a) use a sans serif font and lots of headings ☐
   b) use a serif font and lots of headings ☐
   c) use a serif font and no headings ☐
   d) use a sans serif font and no headings. ☐

7. Giving each page a title is:
   a) unnecessary; they can see what it's about ☐
   b) a nice idea if you are creative ☐
   c) important; do it ☐
   d) extravagant; it takes up too much space. ☐

8. You need to update your website:
   a) regularly ☐
   b) never ☐
   c) we've not got a website to update ☐
   d) I'll ask. I'm not sure. ☐

9. After writing text for the website:
   a) the website goes live immediately ☐
   b) if I have time, a colleague may check it ☐
   c) the website goes down; what did I do wrong? ☐
   d) check the text to make sure it is clear and accurate. ☐

10. I use social media in my work:
    a) for a laugh ☐
    b) never ☐
    c) to interact with potential and existing clients ☐
    d) as the only means of business communication. ☐

SUNDAY MONDAY TUESDAY WEDNESDAY THURSDAY FRIDAY SATURDAY

How to thrive in a tough economic climate

During an economic recession, good business communication becomes even more important. Organizations that recognize that good communication is essential for business are more likely to survive and prosper than those that do not. Managers in organizations that value communication know that good working relationships help morale in the company and make the organization run more smoothly. More than that, good communication also enables business with external clients not only to be maintained but also to be developed. As a manager, your role in ensuring good communication is critical. As well as being the support for the team below you, you are also the channel for passing information from higher in the organization. Here are ten crucial tips to help you make sure that you are an effective communicator in tough times:

1 Work hard at good business relationships

Be aware it's sometimes a matter of not so much what you know as who you know. Good networking and keeping up with contacts – both face to face and online – can sometimes be even more useful than your qualifications and experience. Work hard to develop trust in existing business relationships in both formal times and informal breaks.

2 Appreciate time is money

Prepare well. Be clear. Check what you write – that the facts are accurate and that the grammar and punctuation are correct. Mistakes are costly to put right later. Manage your time as effectively as you can. Make every minute count.

3 Listen well

Listening means not only that you affirm and value other people but also that you can discern how receptive someone is to a new idea and what you are trying to communicate. Furthermore, by listening, you can detect new industry trends and potential gaps in the market.

4 Know your aims

Be crystal clear on what the purpose of your email, report, meeting, presentation or website is. If necessary, discuss this with colleagues and refine it so much that you can summarize your purpose in 12 words.

5 Know your audience

Focus on them, not on yourself. What do you know about the colleague(s) you are trying to communicate to? How much do they know about what you are trying to communicate to them? Put yourself in their shoes as you begin to prepare an email, report, presentation or website. Where do you want them to be as a result of your communication?

6 Know your message

Think exactly what it is that you are trying to communicate. Then, having worked out your key message, break it down into small steps. Anticipate any objections the colleague(s) you are talking or writing to might raise; prepare for them in advance.

7 Know what response you want

Know what response you want from the person you are communicating to, whether it is in an email, report, presentation, website or an item in a meeting. What are the next steps you want them to take? Make it as easy as possible for them to know what the next steps are on how you want them to respond.

8 Communicate using a variety of methods

Choose the best medium for your message, e.g. email, phone or face to face. Email is a good all-round medium but is not the only way. Phoning is good to check someone has understood your message and also to build relationships. If you have to break difficult news, face to face is best. Don't rely only on email; use a range of ways of communicating.

9 Be authentic, real, genuine

Be yourself. People respond to other people, not to contrived techniques that you've read in a book. What is your own special unique contribution that you bring to your email, report, meeting, presentation or website?

10 Spend time fashioning your words carefully and skilfully.

Make sure your content says exactly what you want it to say and that all your steps are logically ordered. Do not give in to the temptation to cut corners and leave a text unedited. Check and revise your email or report before you press 'send'. Check that the tone and level of formality/informality is appropriate to your message.

Answers

Sunday: 1c; 2d; 3c; 4a; 5b; 6b; 7a; 8b; 9c; 10d.

Monday: 1c; 2d; 3b; 4a; 5b; 6c; 7d; 8c; 9c; 10a.

Tuesday: 1b; 2c; 3d; 4a; 5d; 6d; 7c; 8b; 9a; 10b.

Wednesday: 1d; 2d; 3b; 4a; 5c; 6b; 7a; 8d; 9c; 10c.

Thursday: 1a; 2d; 3b; 4b; 5a; 6c; 7d; 8d; 9a; 10c.

Friday: 1b; 2c; 3d; 4d; 5a; 6c; 7b; 8b; 9a; 10d.

Saturday: 1c; 2a; 3d; 4b; 5b; 6a; 7c; 8a; 9d; 10c.

Notes

ALSO AVAILABLE IN THE 'IN A WEEK' SERIES

For information about other titles in the series, please visit
www.inaweek.co.uk